Four Museums

AF134435

Four Museums

Carlo Scarpa, Museo Canoviano, Possagno
Frank O. Gehry, Guggenheim Bilbao Museoa
Rafael Moneo, The Audrey Jones Beck Building, MFAH
Heinz Tesar, Sammlung Essl, Klosterneuburg

Texts
Stefan Buzas
Judith Carmel-Arthur
Kurt W. Forster
Gottfried Knapp
Martha Thorne

Photographs
Joe C. Aker
Richard Bryant
Ralph Richter
Christian Richters
Gary Zvonkovic

Edition Axel Menges

© 2004 Edition Axel Menges, Stuttgart/London
ISBN 3-930698-68-4

All rights reserved, especially those of translation into other languages.

Reproductions: Gábor Mocsonoky, Budapest, and Bild & Text Joachim Baun, Fellbach
Printing and binding: Daehan Printing & Publishing Co., Ltd., Sungnam, Korea

Translation into English: Michael Robinson
Design: Axel Menges

Carlo Scarpa, Museo Canoviano, Possagno
6 Judith Carmel-Arthur and Stefan Buzas: Canova and Scarpa in Possagno
16 Plans
22 Pictorial section with photographs by Richard Bryant

Frank O. Gehry, Guggenheim Bilbao Museoa
60 Kurt W. Forster: The museum as civic catalyst
66 Plans
76 Pictorial section with photographs by Ralph Richter
110 Credits

Rafael Moneo, The Audrey Jones Beck Building, Museum of Fine Arts, Houston
112 Martha Thorne: Reading between the lines: the museums of Rafael Moneo
122 Plans
128 Pictorial section with photographs by Joe C. Aker and Gary Zvonkovic
164 Credits

Heinz Tesar, Sammlung Essl, Klosterneuburg
168 Gottfried Knapp: Raumfiguren für die Kunst – Heinz Tesars Museumsbau für die Sammlung Essl in Klosterneuburg
169 Gottfried Knapp: Spatial figures for art – Heinz Tesar's museum building for the Essl Collection in Klosterneuburg
178 Plans
186 Pictorial section with photographs by Christian Richters
222 Credits

Judith Carmel-Arthur
Canova and Scarpa in Possagno

»The real world is a jumble of awesome complexity and immeasurable charm. Even the inorganic world of rocks and stones is a boundless wonder. Add to that the ingredient of life and the wonder is multiplied beyond imagination ...« (Peter Atkins, *The Periodic Kingdom*.)

These sentences, quoted from a scientist's writings, come to mind when confronted with miraculous effects of light and form, be they due to nature's infinite richness, or to the boundless imagination and creative skill of great artists. In the small addition to the Canova Museum in the village of Possagno, lying in the hills near Treviso in the Veneto, the Italian architect Carlo Scarpa exhibited this boundless wonder of light without which neither life nor art could exist.

Scarpa was commissioned in 1955 by the Superintendent of Fine Arts, Venice, to design this small extension to the existing, early-19th-century Canova plaster-cast gallery and to reposition statuary from the museum's overcrowded collections. Completed in 1957, the extension has a timeless and dramatic quality. The Canova Museum was already remarkable in presenting the collective works of a single individual. With the new extension the museum became – at that time – a unique amalgamation of the Neoclassical and the modern, the old and the new, in uncommon harmony. Both Scarpa's addition and the original 1830s galleries are bathed in rays of natural sunlight which animate the agile forms and refined surfaces of Canova's sculpture.

The extension was meant to function in two significant ways. The first was as a timely regional, if not national commemoration of the late-18th-century Italian sculptor, Antonio Canova (1757–1822), born in Possagno and also entombed there in the Neoclassical »Tempio Canoviano« resting on the summit of Possagno's hill. In 1955 the 200th anniversary of Canova's birth was imminent, and a sympathetic enlargement of the rich, but somewhat restricted spaces of the existing plaster-cast gallery was envisaged as an appropriate tribute. Scarpa's extension, in empirical terms, was also founded in the practical necessity of augmenting the permanent exhibition space of the existing galleries, amplifying and rationalising the display of this unrivalled surviving collection. The new extension would exhibit Canova's many original plaster casts – unusual in their raw power which is often lost in the final polished marbles – in addition to a selection of smaller works, preparatory sketches and *modelli* fabricated in terracotta or sculpted of marble, hitherto accommodated largely in storage rooms.

»Classicism favoured nature idealised in antique form rather than nature natural.« (J. Mordant Crook, *The Greek Revival*)

Journeying to the Museo Canoviana is nothing short of a pilgrimage to experience first-hand the most exquisite traditions of Italian design surviving from the distant and more recent past. Travelling in a northwesterly direction away from Venice, minor roads lead through the small town of Castelfranco, then climb onwards towards the pretty hill town of Asolo where cool winds and rich greenery offer summer retreat from the lagooned city. Caressing wooded hills, the winding roads emerge into an open valley. Distant hills suddenly appear towards the north with the higher reaches of the towering Dolomites in the further distance. In the picturesque greenery of the nearer foothills lies, somewhat unexpectedly, the harmonious fabric of a honey-coloured, domed temple bearing the unmistakable profile of the Roman Pantheon. Turning left from Ascolo is the small village of Possagno, within the shadow of Monte Grappa, mostly and sadly remembered for the dreadful battles fought there in 1917 between Italy and the invading armies of Austria.

Entering Possagno, mountains of stacked bricks and clay shards betray the ancient local traditions of earth-bound craftsmanship. An upper road leads to a broad straight avenue projecting upwards as the »backbone« of the Possagno hill. At its peak lies the unusual, domed temple glimpsed earlier from the distance. This Pantheon-like structure is the Tempio Canoviano, begun in 1819 and originally planned as the village's new parish church, but soon chosen as the final resting place of Possagno's most famous son. Its conception and indeed the very intervention of its Neoclassical design into the traditional architectural character of this quiet village were due to Canova himself.

The structure was conceived by Canova, and its construction initiated at his own expense. Incomplete at the time of his death in 1822, the Temple was finished in 1830 under the instruction of his half-brother and sole heir, the Abate Giovanni Battista Sartori (1775 to 1858). The building was a monumental architectural expression of contemporary Neoclassical design, the late-18th-century style which Canova championed and which his sculpture is so often quoted as embodying in its purest sense.

Leaving the Temple, a lively flight of steps descends to a path leading back towards the village. Across the path is an unremarkable, white stucco-rendered house with shuttered windows. Building forms and superbly crafted local materials of wood, stone and terracotta speak of the modest, domestic architectural traditions of the Veneto. Here there is a large and arched stone entrance and, above, a rectangular panel framed by laurel garlands identifies this as the birthplace of Antonio Canova. An additional notice inscribed with large Roman lettering and set between the windows announces the presence of the »Gypsotheca Museo Canoviano«. Enticed through a modest, arched doorway, one enters the long arcaded passageway and inner courtyard, and from there into one of the most subtle and pleasurable museums even in this so art-filled land.

The early history of the museum is instructive. Following Canova's death in 1822, as the sculptor's sole heir Giovanni Battista Sartori had the contents of Canova's vast studio in Rome transported to Possagno. There Canova had also kept a studio at the family home. Together, surviving artefacts from both locations formed the nucleus of the present museum. They included a multitude of plaster casts, unfinished and unsold marble sculptures, *modelli* and sculptural sketches fabricated of terracotta and wax, and a selection of two-dimensional works including drawings, watercolours, and tempera paintings on black ground, in addition to working tools and personal momenti. By 1832 Sartori commissioned the architect Francesco Lazzari to construct a museum on the family's property, adjacent to the house where Canova was born, in order to

1. Antonio Selva, Tempio Canoviano, Possagno, 1819 to 1830. (Photo: Richard Bryant.)

preserve this extraordinary collection. The first plaster-cast gallery was thus accommodated in Lazzari's Neoclassical building completed in 1836, with its tripartite basilica plan, imposing coffered vaults, and large clerestory windows which flood the three interior galleries with an abundance of diffuse light. The first »keeper« of the Canova collections chosen by Sartori was the Possagno sculptor »Tonin« Pasino who bore Canova's own nickname. By 1853 Sartori had also established the predecessor of the present Canova Foundation to which he legally bequeathed his half-brother's immovable assets.

Unfortunately, the present text is not long enough to afford a full examination of the rich potential offered by the collections in the Museo Canoviano. However it is worthwhile offering some observations about the nature of those collections, thus establishing something of a context for further comments. The first of these observations is the often overlooked fact that the act itself of sculpting is a demanding and rigorous physical process; one requiring great precision, strength and manual skill. The sheer physical beauty of Canova's work perhaps all to readily disguises the long hours of labour and technical authority each finished work entailed. Contemporary sculptural procedures were outlined and illustrated by line drawings in the practical handbook, *Istruzione Elementare per gli Studiosi della Scultura*, published by Francesco Carradori in 1802, an invaluable source for understanding Canova's production techniques.

At Possagno, as the museum's catalogue affirms, it is possible to follow the many individual stages of Canova's method, beginning with the choice and use of tools, the drawings or painted preparatory sketches, the making of wax and terracotta sketches in which he first expressed his compositional or figural ideas, and then the full-sized clay models from which the plaster casts were taken, and lastly the creation of the marble statues achieved – in the concluding stages – with the aid of artificial light thrown from candles used to illuminate the many subtleties of surface modulation.

The plaster casts were a crucial moment in this process. They committed the final sculptural idea to a full-scale format. Key points along their three-dimensional surfaces were then marked, or »pointed«, with small nails, and exact measurements taken from between these points and transferred to the marble, allowing studio apprentices to then block out the final figure before Canova himself applied the finishing touches. Several references in Canova's diaries record the number of hours he worked on the originals, and those hours of his assistants in the heavy labour of fixing the plaster casts and carving marble blocks which eventually emerged as the master's finished compositions.

A second observation is that a working sculpture studio in late-18th-century Rome was a site not only of production, but also of consumption. Patrons and potential clients visited the artist's studio to view works in progress and, whilst there, negotiate possible works for the future. The studio also offered a glimpse of

smaller works, studies, *modelli* and sketches reflecting the unique processes of artistic invention. Other and perhaps competing patrons' commissions might be glimpsed during execution, spurring desire to engage the master's future services for one's own pleasure and edification. The studio functioned as a sort of showroom of past, present and potential projects, clearly taking on an added »sales« factor.

It is indeed rare in the history of 18th-century sculpture that the contents of such a renowned artist's studio should survive so fully intact. It is due to the vision of Sartori that such a resource remains available to inspire further study not only of Canova, but also of the intricate relationships between sculpted artefacts from the period, processes of their making and the contemporary climate of patronage. The collections at Possagno allow rare insight into the nature of sculpture as a working profession.

But what are some further implications for the museum of Sartori's foresight and generous benefaction? Lying at the heart of his original impulse to preserve Canova's possessions for posterity there is the conception of a »collection« as a »bastion against the deluge of time«.

Sartori's decision to maintain the studio artefacts intact as a group effectively rescued that store of objects from dispersal and possible loss. The act of establishing a permanent collection can be viewed in retrospect as a gesture of salvation – especially of vulnerable smaller modelli and terracotta sketches – from the natural ravages of time and changing tastes.

The museum's collection is not a complete »set« in that it does not provide a definitive *catalogue raisonné*, but it is monographic – that is, of Canova only. By preserving the artefacts of a single artist as a sustained group, and by ensuring their survival under the auspices of a Canova »foundation«, Sartori in effect took it upon himself to »construct« how history – in retrospect – would view his famous half-brother. Posterity largely sees Canova triumphal, as he is presented to us by the museum. As a result of the museum being what and where it is, our perception of Canova is also totalizing. Visiting the museum, we experience him from birth, through life, up to the moment of his death. He is presented to us ready-ordered. But this is not necessarily a criticism. On the contrary, in the end we are invited to travel through the various phases of the artist's life and his career, in consequence coming to know him more deeply, more heroically.

Antonio Canova was born in Possagno on 1 November 1757. Early important sources about him include the first catalogue of his works by Tadini (*Le sculture e le pitture di Antonio Canova pubblicate fino a quest' anno 1795*) published in Venice in 1796. Around the time of Canova's death two further sources were published, one the exhaustive 14 volume catalogue in the form of an opera completa by Teotochi Albrizzi – *Opere di scultura e di plastica di Antonio Canova* (Pisa, 1821-24) and the second biography by Paravia – *Notizie intorno alla vita di Antonio Canova* (Venice, 1822).

Shortly afterwards, Canova's own close friends and associates contributed to the growing eulogies of the artist, including two separate volumes by the Italian historian of sculpture, Count Leopoldo Cicognara – *Biografia di Antonio Canova* (Venice, 1823); *Storia della scultura dal suo risorgimento in Italia fino al secolo di Canova* (Prato, 1824) and the influential volume by the French theorist and historian Quatremère de Quincy – *Canova et ses ouvrages* (Paris, 1834). Such sumptuous *compendia*, some including expensive line engravings of the works, published so shortly after the artist's death attest to the high cultural significance Canova was already seen to have attained.

Canova's life offers a biography ruled by an exuberant desire to create, although its details are relatively simple ones. To list, to describe and to evaluate his vast number of sculptures – including some 60 portrait busts close on 40 statues, and over a dozen figural groups – is beyond the scope of this text which intends only to tell his story in abbreviated form. Even this modest account, however, easily betrays the rapid progress towards critical recognition which his talent came to enjoy.

Canova's father, Pietro, was a local stonemason of some repute who died in 1761 when the young Antonio was just 3 years old. One year later his mother married Francesco Sartori of the neighbouring village of Crespano, leaving her first son to be raised in Possagno by his paternal grandfather Passino, also a stonemason and sculptor of modest religious monuments. Her son by this second marriage was Giovanni Battista Sartori, Canova's half-brother, lifelong friend and the sole executor of his estate.

Canova's grandfather may have been the first to detect the child's unusual natural affinity to stone. By the early 1770s Canova had left Possagno for Venice where he would receive a traditional artistic education, and where his pronounced natural ability would first win favour within the ranks of the patriciate. He was apprenticed to the sculptor Giuseppe Bernardini, but was later present in the workshop of the sculptor Giovanni Ferrari. He is known to have carefully studied works in the collections of the Accademia, often drawing there, and perhaps more significantly to have often studied the well-known plaster casts after the antique in the famous collection of Filippo Farsetti. Goethe had visited that collection in the 1770s, and admired it as one of the most comprehensive of the latter 18th century.

At this time, such collections of plaster-cast replicas after celebrated antique originals remained largely in private hands. But permission could be obtained, as Canova did, to study them by freely sketching and making carefully measured drawings. By the late 1700s, cast galleries had become more important than ever in the training of future artists. They encouraged methodical stylistic analysis, and remained a main source for study of the human figure in action and repose. They were also the most valuable available source for promoting knowledge of classical statuary, busts and reliefs. For Canova, the Farsetti collection was an invaluable early source, equivalent in its impact upon him to the sculpture collections of Rome which he would later study.

The patronage network to which he gained access in Venice can equally not be underestimated. Canova subsequently produced a significant tomb monument for Pope Clement XIII, cousin of the Farsetti family. Some of his earliest works in marble were already recognised for their technical virtuosity, such as the two *Baskets of Fruit* of 1774 now in the Museo Correr which were given pride of place along the landing of Farsetti's Venetian palace. A terracotta copy, now in the Accademia in Venice, of Farsetti's plaster cast of the acclaimed

antique *Wrestlers* amongst the collection of the Tribuna of the Uffizi Gallery, Florence, then won for Canova a prestigious 2nd prize at the Accademia. These were the first indications of the great works to come, and the type of patronage network in which Canova would rapidly become a major player. Few artists would express themselves in such an explosion of creativity in a succession of great commissions.

Canova went on to produce a series of important figural commissions through the 1770s, being nominated for membership in the Accademia by 1779. His key early works, such as the individual stone figures of *Orpheus and Eurydice* (both 1775–77) and the marble composition of *Daedalus and Icarus* (1778/79) show exceptional maturity and the young master's rapid stylistic evolution away from a vigorous, late-Baroque manner towards more reticent and complex compositions informed by his study of the antique. His work also began to show a more mature play of contrasts between Venetian naturalism and classical idealization.

»As men cannot rise above their principles, so the artists of Greece never rose above the religious and moral sentiments of the age. Their Ideal was that of youth, grace and beauty, thought, dignity and power. Form consequently, as the expression of Mind, was what they chiefly aimed at, and in this way they reached perfection ...« (Lord Lindsay, *Sketches in the History of Christian Art*, 3 vols, London, 1947, I, pp. XIV–XV.)

By the autumn of 1779, Canova was in Rome, intending the visit to be a study of masterpieces of the past. His own record of his travels, and his first impressions of the city are found in his *I Quaderni di Viaggio, 1779–1780* (Venice, 1959). He went on to visit Naples, and the recent excavations at Herculaneum (from 1739) and Pompeii (from 1748), as well as Paestum, Caserta and Charles III's new museum for antiquities at Portici (1750). The figurative frescoes of Pompeii became a lasting inspiration for painterly diversions throughout his life. But it was Rome, with its confluence of artists from the many centres of Europe, which gave him firm understanding and true empathy with art of the classical past.

By the late 18th century Rome was an obligatory pilgrimage for any serious aspiring artist. This was the city »where it is hardly to be believed what is constantly being found in Rome and its surroundings, for barely a day passes without one coming across a statue, a cameo, an engraved stone, a precious piece of marble ...« (Anatole de Montaiglon, ed., *Correspondance*, 18 vols, Paris 1887–1912, VIII, p. 324.) This was the age of the Grand Tour. Celebrated antiquities located in and around the city had become a glowing presence in the minds of Europe's elite, educated and wealthy arbiters of taste. What is more, knowledge of the ancients was a kind of nourishment to contemporary culture, and was virtually a pre-requisite for modernity in the arts.

Such knowledge was best acquired first-hand through studying the city's famous artefacts, as Canova set himself to do. But much was also to be gained through brushing shoulders with Rome's community of artists, connoisseurs and archaeological scholars who themselves possessed or had access to the city's acclaimed sculpture collections. These included Canova's subsequent associates, the British archaeologist and art dealer Gavin Hamilton (1723–1798), and the British collector Sir William Hamilton (1730–1803), both of whom shared Canova's passion for the antique and his sensibility for the emerging style of Neoclassicism.

However, it was the antiquaries resident in Rome, notably Johann Joachim Winckelmann (1717–1768), librarian to renowned antiquities collector Cardinal Alessandro Albani, who devoted genuine scholarship to the study of the antique. Under Winckelmann's immense influence, an understanding of classical Greek art was placed on firmer archaeological footing for the first time, while appreciation of the classical past increasingly looked to Greek statuary to reveal inspiration for essential human values of beauty, truth, and liberty – values already heralded by the age of the Enlightenment. Winckelmann's claim that the emerging »Neoclassical« ideal of beauty was one of »noble grace and quiet grandeur«, aligned Neoclassicism with the perceived delicacy and *finesse* of Greek statuary, rather Roman, and carried inestimable authority for young artists such as Canova.

When Canova later journeyed to London, he especially marvelled at the exquisite statuary from the Parthenon in Athens. The Elgin Marbles are that much more remarkable in their superb treatment for having originally comprised nearly fifty separate figures, some of colossal scale, others over life-size. They were originally positioned in the temple's metopes and pediments, well above eye level, and therefore viewed not straight-on, but from an oblique angle well below. Canova wrote to his friend Quatremere de Quincy on 9 November 1815 »... Here I am in London, dear and best friend, a wonderful city ... I have seen the marbles arrived from Greece. Of the basreliefs we had some idea from engravings, but of the full colossal figures, in which an artist can display his whole power and science, we have known nothing ... The figures of Phidias are all real and living flesh, that is to say, are beautiful nature itself.« What Canova so potently recognised in the Elgin Marbles only confirmed the realisation of his youth, that »living flesh, beautiful nature itself« was to be his life's aim, and that these qualities, through his prodigious talent could be realised through the grandiose language of the classical tradition.

But the »true style« of Neoclassicism, so-called by its most ardent defenders in Rome, was essentially a backlash against the exuberance of the Baroque. And the term »Neoclassicism«, coined in the mid-19th century, is difficult to define and remains something of a misnomer or – in the least – a debatable descriptive reference. Broadly speaking, the style was at the very heart of a new apparatus of taste. It was a synthesis of intellectual classicism with romantic naturalism, adding to these a genuine interest in recent archaeological discoveries which empirically demonstrated what was classically »correct«.

Neoclassicism, nonetheless, quickly became associated with mere stylism and more with modish decoration than with the aspirational »new Renaissance« so ardently embraced by its purist advocates, including the young Antonio Canova. In the same sense, Canova's sculptures represent far more within the history of sculpture than his original great fame – as a »Neoclassical« artist – alone could do. For Canova, his presence in Rome was nothing less than a dynamic engagement with the most influential artistic and theoretical developments of his day, and it was the richness of this experience coupled with his intrinsic gifts which led him to be far more than a mere imitator after the antique.

Canova remained in Rome, and by the early 1780s began to produce more mature and sophisticated compositions. The artefacts in the Gypsoteca Canoviano provide an excellent representative chronology of this aesthetic development. Although the museum contains mainly preparatory works, with comparatively few finished marbles, it remains possible to map the highlights of his œuvre by reviewing the collections.

In Rome, Canova began to design a series of innovative funerary monuments which progressively employed less robust, quieter and more sacramental imagery than their late-Baroque precedents. These works also expressed Winckelmann's new ideals of quiet elegance and repose. They included the monument to Clement XIV; that for Clement XIII; the unexecuted monument to the Venetian painter Titain; and the plaster cast from 1817–22 of Pius VI.

The most important of these grandiose compositions is represented in Possagno by the large-scale plaster cast of 1800 for the funerary monument of Maria Christina of Austria. Here Canova brought about a powerful fusion of bold architectural motifs with the human figure. The radically new compositional scheme, developed from the earlier monument to Titian, focused around the architecture of the tomb itself, its severe pyramidal form rising fatefully upwards behind the figures which are aligned in a processional cortege near the tomb's open door. The figures' gestures are reticent; their idealization learned from classical models.

One of Canova's most delicate, popular and admired subjects was the theme of *Cupid and Psyche*, executed in both single figures and in more technically demanding group compositions from the mid-1780s. As much as anything, his work in the genre established him as the 18th-century's master of this erotic-mythological category. At Possagno there is a fine terracotta sketch of 1787 for the famous finished marbles representing reclining figures of *Amor and Psyche* in the Hermitage. There is also a plaster cast dating from around 1800 of a standing *Cupid and Psyche* group. This work already shows the complex intermingling of form and a relaxed sensuality of individual gestures. Although the cast indicates only one of Canova's formulations of this subject, the Neoclassical ideal of sensuality, lightness and graceful charm is wholly personified in the daring yet balletic pose of the nude adolescent male, a tangible realisation of Winckelmann's aesthetic maxims. Other works at Possagno within this genre include the complex plaster cast of 1789 representing *Adone Wreathed by Venus*, and the standing group of *Venus and Ado*.

As Canova continued to explore the expressive potential inherent in classical subjects, he also refined his interest in themes of masculine strength and pugilism, exploring tensions between irrational Dionysian forces and rational Apollonian virtue. During much of his life commissions for over life-size mythological figures added to his fame and popularity. Works of this type show Canova's mastery in acknowledging precedent, such as that of the celebrated antique *Farnese Hercules*. Sculptors through history have consciously looked to sculpture of the past in order to determine their own boundaries. Sculpture references sculpture, and Canova's approach was no different. But while displaying erudition, he was equally concerned to reinterpret psychological states of turmoil with a new heroic restraint which was completely modern, original, and artistically challenging. At Possagno, works of this type include the statue of the pugilist Damoxenos, and the remarkable plaster cast dating from 1795 to 1815 of the over life-size mythological group of *Hercules and Licus* with its complex triangular outline, a work of exceptionally subtle impact.

Other works surviving at Possagno represent Canova's gifts as a portraitist. Especially after the turn of the century his portrait sculpture gained considerable praise, and was sought after in many European courts. Far more commissions were proposed than could be attempted or completed, and much survives executed in both marble and plaster cast. Canova had the rare ability to model facial character and drapery with an alluring naturalism, but at the same time moderating this with a compositional formality rooted in antique Roman portraiture.

Canova accepted a number of important commissions for allegorical-cum-portrait sculpture, producing some exemplary large-scale statues which prove his ability to reinterpret antique prototypes in a modern idiom. Amongst the works surviving at Possagno are the plaster cast of the imposing figure of *Madame Mère, Leitzia Ramolino*, Napoleon's mother, the original marble now in the Duke of Devonshire's collection at Chatsworth in Derbyshire. In this case the antiquel formulae for sovereign power – a hierarchical depiction of Emperor or Empress presiding rigidly upright and frontal – has been mediated by the feigned grace and languidness of contemporary taste. Canova's statuary responded to the politics of patronage on this and many other occasions.

Canova also designed a number of reclining figures mimicking, while not reproducing antique prototypes. Further, his large scale, heroic statuary was perhaps less portraiture strictly speaking than an exercise in satisfying the market for political memorials. There are several excellent preparatory works for this type of statuary at Possagno, including the plaster model depicting George Washington enthroned in the antique manner of a lawmaker.

One must not omit the considerable number of marble and cast-plaster compositions in bas-relief when recounting Canova's œuvre. Produced from the late 1780s onward, many surviving at Possagno, these works are in some respects closer to painting than sculpture. They emphasise Canova's exploration of purely sculptural relationships between figure and background, as well as his continuing interest in the potential of sculpture to tell a story. Drawing their abundant subjects from Greek mythology and tragedy, as well as from the Old and New Testaments, their format is based upon the conventional geometry of antique, primarily Attic Greek stelae. In Canova's hands compositions such the bas-relief for Nicola Antonio Giustiniani became exceptionally lively and powerful.

Amongst the more than one dozen sculpted figural groups executed by Canova, *The Three Graces* exemplifies his deep understanding of the human body and its infinite subtleties of movement. Carved for the Empress Josephine, it is perhaps the most famous of his works. Such creations belie the often held opinion that the Neoclassical vision of Canova could be cold, its intentions merely »skin deep«. Canova's treatment of the theme is anything but impersonal. The graceful intertwining of figures in this revolving composition shows the delicacy with which Canova was able to interlock apparently living forms in contrapuntal harmony. The ef-

2. Antonio Canova, *The Three Graces*, 813–16. (Photo: Richard Bryant.)

fortless transition between one figure and another absorbs the spectator, drawing the eye into the deceptive simplicity of the figural group. In his biographical memoir of the sculptor published in 1824, Count Cicognara observed the elegant forms and tender embraces of the figures, and how gently a play of light animates their surfaces.

The plaster-cast for *The Three Graces* now stands superbly positioned in the Scarpa wing of the museum. Its pristine state invites the viewer to contemplate Canova's sensual expression of Winckelmann's maxim of »noble simplicity and quiet grandeur«, and to genuinely appreciate the sentiment and technical virtuosity which produced such sculptural rhythm and figural poise, raising this superbly crafted sculpture into a masterpiece of its period.

During the course of his remarkable career, Canova had periodically journeyed to Possagno. Towards the end of his life, suffering chronic illness, he finally returned there, devoting the last years of his life to the design and construction of the noble Neoclassical-style Temple. Construction began under the supervision of the architect Antonio Selva, and Canova himself laid the foundation stone in an elaborate ceremony on 11 July 1819. Within the church there is Canova's last major work.

A year before his death he was engaged on a large funerary monument dedicated to the Marchese di Salza, but little could he have known that his own funerary monument would shortly be constructed from this unfinished composition, and would shelter his own body and that of his half-brother. Antonio Canova died on 13 October 1822. At the time of his death in 1822 no living sculptor in Europe could command the immense admiration, and sometimes disparagement, which Canova had received during the course of his lifetime.

Having attempted to describe the remarkable talent, vision and knowledge of one exceptional man, it is now necessary to try to define the rare creative gifts of another, equally exceptional man. But as much as any true architect, because Carlo Scarpa's creativity sprang from his personal response to the subtle variables of light and spatial interplay, no publication can satisfactorily represent the indefinable balance he was able to achieve between dark and light, void and solid, volume and mass. It is almost impossible to transmit such values effectively in words.

Even the finest of Scarpa's compositions can only remain pleasurable, long after, to the viewer who is intimately and subconsciously aware of Scarpa's fusion of space and the object with light. To convey the magical qualities of his work, even the mythical power of the written word can only give some modest revelation. Richard Bryant's photographs included here come nearest to revealing Scarpa's personal world of intense beauty.

Scarpa's ways of working were perhaps nearer those of architects from past centuries. He did not require either the technical facilities or the fast-paced, professionally organised routine which we so readily associate with architectural practice in the present day. His designs – of which there remains an archive of over 18,000 drawings – were largely executed during the quiet hours of the night, while daytime was reserved for the pleasurable activities of reading and looking, and enjoying a constant discourse with friends and associates. Young and not so young colleagues joined him from many countries to benefit from his cultured approach, and assisted in executing drawings for the realisation of his designs. But in the end there has never been any question that all Scarpa's designs were his and his alone. For Scarpa was renowned for his intuitive skills in transforming through drawing any idea into living matter. The nearest one can come to understanding the complex inception and development of his ideas is to study those drawings.

A native Venetian, Scarpa was born in 1906. The impact of the place of his birth on the manner in which he conceived of architecture cannot be underestimated. By self-definition a craftsman, a problem solver and a maker of interventions in the built environment, Scarpa saw inert form as being infused with life through its discreet dialogues with materials, space, and above all light and time. For Scarpa, the changing shape of light creates the shape of things. Shifting intensities of volume, mass, texture and colour are dependent upon the resonances of light, and materiality is achieved alongside the ephemeral and the transparent. There is a Venetian pedigree to these empowered notions of light, time and transformation, and this pedigree is ever present in Scarpa's Œuvre.

It is possible here only to briefly summarise Scarpa's career with a focus upon some of those moments which contributed most to his eminent achievements at Possagno between 1955 and 1957. Scarpa initially trained at the renowned Accademia di Belle Arti in Venice in architectural design. Although he never obtained his licence, he enjoyed a lengthy and influential teaching career from 1926 at Venice's Istituto Universitario di Architettura, eventually obtaining the distinction of professor. Beginning in the following year he worked as a professional designer, and continued to run a design studio through the early 1960s.

In 1927 Scarpa obtained the prestigious post of artistic consultant to the Murano glass manufacturer Capellini, subsequently taking up a post of the same title with the famous Venini firm on Murano in 1933 and remaining there until 1947. Scarpa's formative designs for Venini glass already effortlessly showed his unique facility for invention, along with his abiding regard for long-established artisinal tradition.

From the beginning, Scarpa maintained a progressive dialogue between crafts conventions and the disciplines of design. His experimental approach sought out the innumerable possibilities offered by materials and methods, and he spared no effort in liasing closely with master craftsmen and artisans with whom he came to form long-lasting co-operations. Acknowledging his collaborators with the highest praise, Scarpa considered himself one of them – an artisan – and often worked with the same masters over many projects. In this, Scarpa tacitly acknowledged the profession of architecture as one of inter-dependent and inter-disciplinary relations.

His focus on this essential exchange was itself an assertion that traditions of »manual craft« were a decisive element in the designing and making of new architecture. This point of view betrayed an equally auspicious approach to all architecture as an ongoing process of new research into the indivisible pursuits of building craft and design. Scarpa's experiences with glassmaking first at Cappellini and then at Venini in part motivated his enquiries into the potentials and limita-

tions of craft convention, and were subsequently recognised as a seminal influence in his developing focus upon problematic combinations of the old with the new. These considerations were soon combined to form his strategy for any intervention in an historic architectural fabric.

By the end of the 1930s, Scarpa had become involved with the restoration of historic structures. Over the following years he would gain immense critical praise for his rejuvenation of the interiors of historic galleries and museums in Italy, his work commissioned by various institutions concerned with not only progressive design, but also the tourist industry. The first instance of this type of intervention was in the ancient historic fabric of the Ca' Foscari in Venice, during 1936/37, where Scarpa's endeavours provided evidence of his consummate skill in the manipulation of materials. This commission also proved Scarpa's sensitivity towards designing structure and space while prioritising the contextual importance of historic artefacts on display. He consistently expressed special concern to retain the authenticity and integrity of any structure. He also looked carefully at the more abstract qualities of atmosphere and light in order to retain the timelessness of any historic fabric in which a collection of artefacts was present, achieving an atmospheric intimacy which evoked the past life of the artefacts themselves and their role in the story of a surviving building.

Prior to his work at the Canoviano in Possagno, Scarpa had also gained experience during 1953/54 in designing the museum interior of the Palazzo Abatellis in Palermo, and was subsequently occupied with similar interventions at the Museo Correr in Venice in 1953 to 1960, and at the Fondazione Querini-Stampalia, also in Venice, in 1961–63. In 1964 Scarpa again achieved critical recognition for his redesign at the Museo Civico di Castelvecchio in Verona, a seminal instance in which the institution was sited in a venerable building being reinvented with mindful regard for its unique past.

Throughout the course of his work in the museum and gallery sector, Scarpa's interventions questioned prevailing notions about museum design and also interrogated the time-honoured idea of galleries as otherworldly spaces secreted within venerable structures often lacking sufficient air or natural light. Scarpa's response to the redesign of such interiors simply addressed different challenges. He looked painstakingly at the whole of a site and its available space. He interpreted artefacts themselves as the active agents to be accommodated foremost in any »exhibition« building scheme. Because Scarpa prioritised the requirements of artefacts, his architectural choices facilitated a new, more purely abstract approach to renovation and intervention, and this is seen perhaps above all at Possagno.

Other early considerations which informed Scarpa's eventual work at the Canova Museum were located in his experimental approach to exhibition display. Part of the success and magic of Possagno rests clearly on the nature of his display solutions which drew together in an entirely new and remarkable fashion much of the experience and expertise gained earlier. His career interrupted by the Second World War, during the late 1940's Scarpa began a series of co-operations with the prestigious Venice Biennale, a relationship which served to bring his work in the field of exhibition and display design to the critical attention of an international audience. From 1948 until 1972 he acted as design consultant to the Biennale, contributing to nine Biennali overall, with a number of acclaimed exhibitions, including that for the works of Paul Klee in 1948, the Book Pavilion in 1950 and the Venezuela Pavilion in 1954–56. In addition to permanent museum installations and the redesign of commercial shops and showrooms, such as his now classic design for Olivetti in the Piazza San Marco (1957/58), Scarpa also designed numerous exhibitions outside of Venice, including the exposition of Mondrian's work in Rome in 1956, and the renowned exhibition of original mural paintings, *Frescoes from Florence*, after the great flood of the Arno in 1966. When that exhibition travelled internationally, other countries received their first glimpse of Scarpa's singular genius in contemporary display design.

For Scarpa, exhibitions, particularly those sited in museums, offered far more than a mere occasion to mediate on behalf of collected artefacts in the illustrious warehouses of European culture. Instead, he conceived of an exhibition as an aesthetic thoroughfare in which all elements of visual culture and the built environment were channelled together. As such, each new exhibition offered the designer a chance to personally assess the artefacts through display design, also bringing new and unexpected insight to bear upon the presentation of works to a viewing public.

Scarpa's manner of both museum and exhibition design drew together various themes. While always acknowledging that environmental design for single and collective artefacts needed to be, certainly in theory, focused upon the immutable factors of space, mass and light, Scarpa equally recognised the same principles as fundamental to architectural expression, and was therefore unforgiving of much traditional museum and gallery design that was not primarily architectural in the first instance. In practical terms, the design of a museum or gallery interior is an intricate affair, requiring refined technical considerations, especially in order to achieve an all-around diffusion of natural light in conventionally top-lit spaces. Scarpa believed the best exhibition designers were those most able to architecturally exploit the complexities of natural light.

To some extent, Scarpa's approach was also an attempt to de-mystify the traditionally reticent museum environment and to provoke a more aware response to the continuum of aesthetic possibilities – past and present – inherent in so many museum settings. To do so he acknowledged the numerous sequences of activities which brought together otherwise separate design possibilities, so that in the end the whole of a building became an exhibit, and a multitude of considerations – structure, volume, colour, and light – were powerfully fused together. In Scarpa's hands, cultural masterpieces assumed a new complexity and their value was renewed, while a building itself could no longer be perceived as inflexible and immune to time, but was rejuvenated by its role in the course of incessant change which he made visible.

The single consistent feature of Scarpa's œuvre which most defies not only analysis, but the power of the written word, is his mastery of light. This mastery was exemplified, above all, in his universally acclaimed eminence in museum and exhibition design. It is therefore appropriate in the present work to celebrate Scarpa's vision by looking closely at one commission in the field of museum and display design which has been consistently heralded in the critical literature as the most

3. Carlo Scarpa, Galleria Nazionale della Sicilia, Palazzo Abatellis, Palermo, 1953/54. (From: Christine Hoh-Slodczyk, *Carlo Scarpa und das Museum*, Berlin, 1987.)
4. Carlo Scarpa, Galleria Fondazione Querini Stampalia, Venice, 1961–63. (From: Christine Hoh-Slodczyk, *Carlo Scarpa und das Museum*, Berlin, 1987.)
5. Carlo Scarpa, Museo Civico di Castelvecchio, Verona, 1956–64. (From: *Global Architecture*, 51.)
6. Carlo Scarpa, Olivetti showroom, Venice, 1957–59. (From: *Global Architecture*, 51.)

outstanding of his masterpieces in this area: the addition he built between 1955 and 1957 in Possagno for the Gipsoteca Canoviana.

In the apparent simplicity of its design, Scarpa's extension at Possagno is both deceptive and ingenious. The existing basilica-like museum was enlarged by a comparatively small addition. Within three distinct and beautifully orchestrated volumes Scarpa was able to create a composition comparable to a musical suite in three movements, also creating a suite in luminosity. It is difficult to describe the abundance of spatial compositions which arise wherever on looks. Suffice it to say that these spaces leave one with a feeling of abundant joy.

The site was originally a narrow, descending plot stretching nearly the entire length of one of the »nave« sides of the existing basilica-like museum. The site thus presented a series of complex variables in respect to both the terrain and the extant structure. Scarpa designed the extension as an irregular »L« shape, consisting of three volumes. The shortest segment of the »L« is attached to the old museum, forming one roughly rectangular gallery along with the cubic »high« gallery. The longest stretch of the »L« is slightly offset from the side of the museum building, running parallel to the larger structure, downwards towards the boundary of the site, and forming an elongated wedge-shaped gallery. Scarpa's design also includes a narrow exterior passageway between the long wedge-shaped gallery and the museum wall. Overall, this arrangement of new, low-lying sequential volumes allows the mass of the 19th-century building to remain dominant and, in comparison, Scarpa's addition is both precious and understated.

Although Scarpa was given complete freedom in the development of his design, and was required to preserve nothing, his plan amounted to a radical modification of the historical site without impeding the integrity of any of the surviving buildings. The new galleries are effectively woven into the original fabric of the site. They are also unobtrusively woven into the existing fabric of the mediaeval hilltown with apparently little effort. Although in part standing free of the museum, the addition is densely packed alongside it and thereby echoes the more traditional associative relationships between generations of existing buildings scattered through in the village.

In addition to the galleries, Scarpa almost imperceptibly added a new boundary wall between the site and the adjacent street. This simple device helped to unobtrusively join his interventions to the local built environment by echoing its own intrinsic irregularity. The wall exemplifies the detailed considerations which Scarpa introduced at every level of his design activity in order to fully integrate the »new« within the urban landscape. The wall also enriches the new gallery wing by articulating Scarpa's interpretation of the traditional walled patio garden as an exterior space both notionally and architecturally integrated with its environment.

Volumetric relationships within Scarpa's design are no less responsive to the problematic site. The new wing is defined by three discrete volumes, each a small gallery. Individually they boast complex relationships with one another, as well as with the existing museum building, the site and the adjacent street.

The exterior of the addition is stucco rendered masonry, with rough concrete finishing around the windows and along the roof line. This quite subtle play of dissimilar surface textures imparts the illusion of change in the perceived scale of separate parts, especially in the juxtaposition of the imposing wall surface with the more delicate detailing around the edges.

The first and largest of these volumes forms a transitional, narrative space between the old and the new. It is a slightly irregular, rectangular gallery with one angled wall, poised immediately off the old museum and the only portion of the new Scarpa wing to be pinned against the original structure.

This top-lit semi-shadowy first area gives a glimpse into the formal arrangement of the lofty basilica. In its centre, Canova's beautiful pyramidal composition representing *Adonis Crowned by Venus* is gently illuminated by a golden-coloured rooflight, this soft source also bestowing an almost tactile quality to the row of female busts. It is also possible from here to look directly into both smaller volumes of the new »L« shaped wing, and forward into the alluring distances of Italian landscape.

This is also the point where all four contrasting spaces meet, tempting one's next direction. With a tantalising view ahead, the second volume begins to reveal itself. This volume is the tall cubic, or »high«, gallery, renowned for its four magnificent corner skylights. To the left down two short flights of steps the third volume comprises the long, wedge-shaped gallery which in its changing levels mirrors the capricious, stepped fall of the natural ridge of the hill as it drops downwards into the rural countryside. At this end of the gallery one comes upon the full-height window that is the one connection with the outside. Here, there is a carefully contrived juxtaposition between architectural structure, sky, trees and Canova's famous group of *The Three Graces*.

Beyond the glazing, the basin of water reflects the sky and supplies a shimmering light from below to counter the strong light from the sky – a memorable invention which imparts a seductive softness to the intertwining forms of *The Three Graces*. In this respect, if in no other, Scarpa was a masterful manipulator of natural light and a descendant of the great Venetian traditions of illumination.

In its blending of old and new, the contemporary with the historic, the first gallery is perhaps the most symbolic. It is the key site in which Scarpa addresses the matter of intervention. Here, along one side of the low-ceilinged room, a former exterior wall of the older museum building is retained and transformed by Scarpa into an exhibition wall for the Canova bas-reliefs. Scarpa also manipulated notions of interior and exterior by creating an »invisible« arcaded passageway down the inside of the wall, alternating the height of the passage with that of the main gallery space, while employing exposed I-beams to form the rhythmic supports of the arcade. Functionally the I-beams mimic classical columns, but their material presence has been made relatively transparent by an overlay of white paint. The meaning of the arcade, however, is not located in the notion of a passageway, but in the positioning of Canova's work along the opposite wall. For a viewer in the gallery, the change of floor level necessitates a pause in motion. The edge of the gallery floor becomes a viewing platform, dictating the most opportune level and distance from which to admire Canova's work. The »invisible« arcade and the viewing platform are architec-

tural devices enabling Scarpa to uncover layers of the building's history in a single narrative moment.

The »invisible« corridor is a primary example at Possagno of how Scarpa experimented with different possible readings of the building as a »container«. Multiple levels of meaning shown in a single architectural moment such as this allowed Scarpa to critically comment on the nature of intervention and to make manifest the principles by which he worked. He is able to offer interpretations in which an historic fabric is veiled or revealed, and to directly address issues of modification and deformation at the same instance in which he preserves a portion of the historic fabric. Slowly journeying through the Possagno galleries, it becomes possible to follow the development of Scarpa's dialogue with the past and to measure such single moments in the story he is telling.

Furthermore, Scarpa's use of monochromatic, white plaster rendering for the interior wall surfaces of this and the other two galleries of the extension was startling in the design of gallery space at that time. The placement of Canova's white plaster and marble artefacts against white walls was a critical response to conventions of sculptural display, while challenging the viewer's perceptions of the subtleties of light, dark and shadow. Scarpa made not only a strongly architectural statement, but one which was perhaps almost painterly in its desire describe in minute detail the subtle transitions of surface volume and texture on both the building and the artefacts.

Scarpa's work at Possagno continues to be regarded as a landmark demonstration of how a highly complex architectural programme involving both the past and the present can be orchestrated. He continues to be admired for his innovations in the overall redesign of the site, down to the most intimate features of the interior. Some of the more subtle features within the galleries, for example, still captivate and marvel, and remain forceful influences of how volumes and artefacts are perceived. Scarpa inserted narrow baseboards of black metal through the new galleries. These radically delineate the junctions between wall and floor, and are unique devices which serve to clarify the individual volumes of the three new galleries, as well as the transitions between them. The baseboards outline the spaces as if by drawn line. In the cubic or »high« gallery Scarpa created a similar effect wherein the surface of the ceiling reaches beyond that of the wall, leaving a narrow inset crevice to fill with shadow, resolutely offsetting the vertical against the horizontal, and causing the ceiling to mysteriously hover.

In its own right, the gallery is a fantastic and lyrical movement in this symphony of light and is a quite remarkable *tour-de-force*. A single step brings one into this enclosed cube, twice the height of the previous space. Such spatial sequence is not unusual. But what is singular, apart from the change in brightness, is the light source. Positioned at each of the upper corners of the cube, four glass rectangles in two matching pairs allow the sky with its moving clouds to illuminate the gleaming white volume of the gallery. The frames of the two longer windows were fabricated from iron, and viewed from the exterior cause the elevation of the stucco-rendered mass to appear changeable. They are supported with slim plaster shelves, bestowing a greater architectonic feeling than apparent in their counterparts. The frames of the smaller cubic windows are obvious only along the vertical contours, while a near invisible triangular member joins the upper glass plate to those at the sides. The result is the entirely unimpeded intrusion of the blue of the Italian sky into the space of the gallery. The surprising, and perhaps even unique invention of the four transparent, inward-penetrating rectangles results in an equally startling condition of natural light.

A normal opening in a wall gives rise to a maximum contrast between the high luminosity of the sky, framed by an almost black edge, to the solid wall surrounding the opening. By inverting this condition and forming transparent membranes of glass, the inward penetration almost totally eliminates harsh contrasts. Surrounding walls are indirectly illuminated, creating a softness that brings the plaster surfaces of Canova's originals to life, caressing the figures. With the sun's rays moving within this luminous cube, angled shafts of sunlight dance along the walls, touching the dramatically placed portrait bust of the sculptor as it is thrust forward on steel brackets, accompanied by a small sketch of Pope Clement XIV below. The whole is an arena of theatrical magic.

The third volume of Scarpa's extension is the »long« or wedge-shaped gallery. Its volume decreases progressively in width as it recedes from the older building, producing a narrow exterior passageway along the wall of the basilica and creating another »spatial« wedge running the length of Scarpa's addition. A glass window-wall of wooden framing comprises that side of the gallery. This simple although radical structural solution within a museum context considerably increases the amount of natural light filling the new gallery, while in part undermining normative interpretations of glass as a mere window onto the outside world. Scarpa not only associates the use of glass with both light and structure, as opposed to view, but employs a contemporary technical solution popularised by the »International« style to express his individual approach to intervention. The window-wall does offer a view, but directly onto the marvellous stuccoed fabric of the 18th-century building With Scarpa, the window is a vehicle through which to examine an architectural fragment, illuminating a different space, a different time, an earlier part of the same narrative. The new offers a telescopic view of the old, and architecture in Scarpa's hands has ceased to be in any way dispassionate. It is self-explanatory, reflecting back upon itself with celebratory intent.

At the far, narrowest end of the gallery, four floor-to-ceiling glass panels were designed with slim, understated vertical supports giving an unimpeded prospect onto the reflecting pool outside. These glass panels bear framing elements only on the inside, allowing the sides of the gallery to deceptively continue unchecked into exterior space. The implementation of this seamless transition was a critical design statement, provoking free visual play from interior to exterior. The result is a remarkable contrast between textures and volumes, suggesting the apparent ease with which Scarpa could interject changes and juxtapositions in materials and meaning within a single plane. By inverting the concept of »edge«, Scarpa unveiled new architectural and symbolic relations between the inside and the outside of the gallery.

Relationships between the relative heights and depths of the galleries are also defined by the significant architectural detailing of the steps and ceilings. Steps

are consistently highlighted as transitional devices, ever leading the spectator into more ethereal worlds. Some are interned by marble sections. All are dramatically undercut, so that the slab stretches outwards horizontally with apparently little or no visible means of support. The most celebrated is the emphatic »floating« step symbolically placed at the entrance to the Scarpa wing. These inventions not only resolve the fundamentally problematic changes of level on the side, but orchestrate the movement of the narrative from old to new.

At Possagno, manipulation of glass by Scarpa was always an emphatic gesture. Glass is present in a selection of sub-narratives, as well as playing a more normative role. It signals the presence of a void, and exacerbates juxtapositions between what is fixed and what is fluid, what is of the present and what endures from the past. It acts as a point of clarification in the observation of Scarpa's design objectives, especially when used as a transparent envelope to intensify perceptions of space and light. The constant movement and mutability of natural light within the galleries also counts amongst the most crucial factors in observing Scarpa's refined positioning of the artefacts.

Scarpa's genius in exhibition design not only exploited his own intrinsic sensibilities, but equally ensued from his recognition of the inherent merits of each work of art. He remained keenly aware of how and where an artefact came into contact with space and light, and designed his means of display around those moments of interaction. Throughout the new galleries the assorted mechanisms of display are invested with diverse measures of reserve. All are poised with self-assurance. Some have a distinctive bearing, while others are entirely more allusive. Whatever their individual character, they offer up solitary stages of the artistic narrative, encouraging a paced, thoughtful journey through the galleries.

One is able to move around displays, getting an intimate sense of sculptural mass and volume. Seductive plays of shadow across solid form become more noticeable, diffuse light illuminates the highly plastic values of the modelling, and profiles are relieved against gradations of light drifting across the background surface of the room. Smaller works have been lifted to a scrupulously judged height. Many are raised upon narrow block stands of polished ebony, its rich dark surface floating against the luminous backdrop of the gallery, the whole effect pulsating in contrasting modulations of light and dark.

Scarpa typically designed each individual stand or platform to perfectly set off a unique artefact, and in reality the props and braces differ markedly in their materials and configurations. Particularly at Possagno the wall-hung exhibits seems to float effortlessly on invisible iron brackets, each strategically placed within a luminous composition of changing light and shadow.

Other supports for smaller statuary are made of masonry, while the large reclining figures are displayed well below eye level on black iron superstructures designed to maintain their weight. The iron and glass vitrines throughout were also designed by Scarpa. Their forms mimic the inward-penetrating lights of the cubic gallery, a delicate black iron armature supporting their floating volumes. They are as transparent as the galleries themselves, and have warranted sustained critical praise.

With Scarpa's interventions, museums also necessarily became centres of contemporary design and as such eclipsed in their possibilities for artistic expression and for learning the more traditional museum enclosure. And all this well before the current emphasis on the so-called »Bilbao phenomenon« gave us museums with »destination« status.

In 1978 Scarpa died in Sendai, Japan. His son Tobia lovingly designed a tomb for his father who was laid to rest at the site of his own architectural *magnum opus*, the Brion Cemetery in San Vito d'Altivole. In *Contemporary World Architecture*, Hugh Pearman wrote, one suspects, with some degree of sentiment that »in the 1970s, it seemed as if one architectural world – the world not only of international modernism, but also of craftsmanship, of conservatism – had died with Scarpa while another world – the world of high-precision, machine-made, radical architecture was taking over«. After setting foot in Possagno, it is impossible to disagree with him.

What is remarkable at Possagno is that the artistic vision of a single architect was so effortlessly able to unite the past with the present, and that the ambiance which resulted intuitively reinforced the aesthetic drama of a valuable corpus of art works. Scarpa's focus on a limited number of materials, perhaps the foremost of these being glass, led to a remarkable uniformity of the structural and aesthetic aims of the project. Possagno has been called one of the 20th Century's finest examples of architectural intervention in an historic fabric. Together with Scarpa's own work at Castelvecchio, it is heralded as less an example of conservation or restoration, than a liberation of architectural meaning and possibility.

During the latter half of the 20th century, increasingly more individuals have journeyed to sites of historic interest, whether they be ancient churches, industrial refurbishments or monuments of rural nostalgia. In the West we suffer an ongoing affair with the historic past. Our passions are, if anything, more acutely engaged after site restoration and conservancy than before. The more frequently, it seems, older structures are preserved, the more frequently we encourage preservation in some form. We perceive ourselves as enthusiastic participants in the ongoing historical narrative, and remain ever keen to personally experience those parts of the story which came before us. Preservation, restoration, and conservation are all factors in the unveiling of the past, and all continue to enrich contemporary knowledge for the benefit of tomorrow.

What Carlo Scarpa unveiled at Possagno, however, was far greater than a moment of the historic past. His unique and crucial contribution was in formulating architectural metaphors by means of which one could more clearly perceive the dynamic of the narrative itself. By so fluidly juxtaposing the old with the new, he allowed buildings to tell the story of history while being active agents of historical progress at the same time.

In this way his contribution is more full-bodied and fertile than conservation or restoration alone could be. His imagination has adapted the past to the present, reversing the customary approach to the renewal of historic architectural monuments, and in doing so enriching our perceptions of what architecture can be. Especially when designed by such a master.

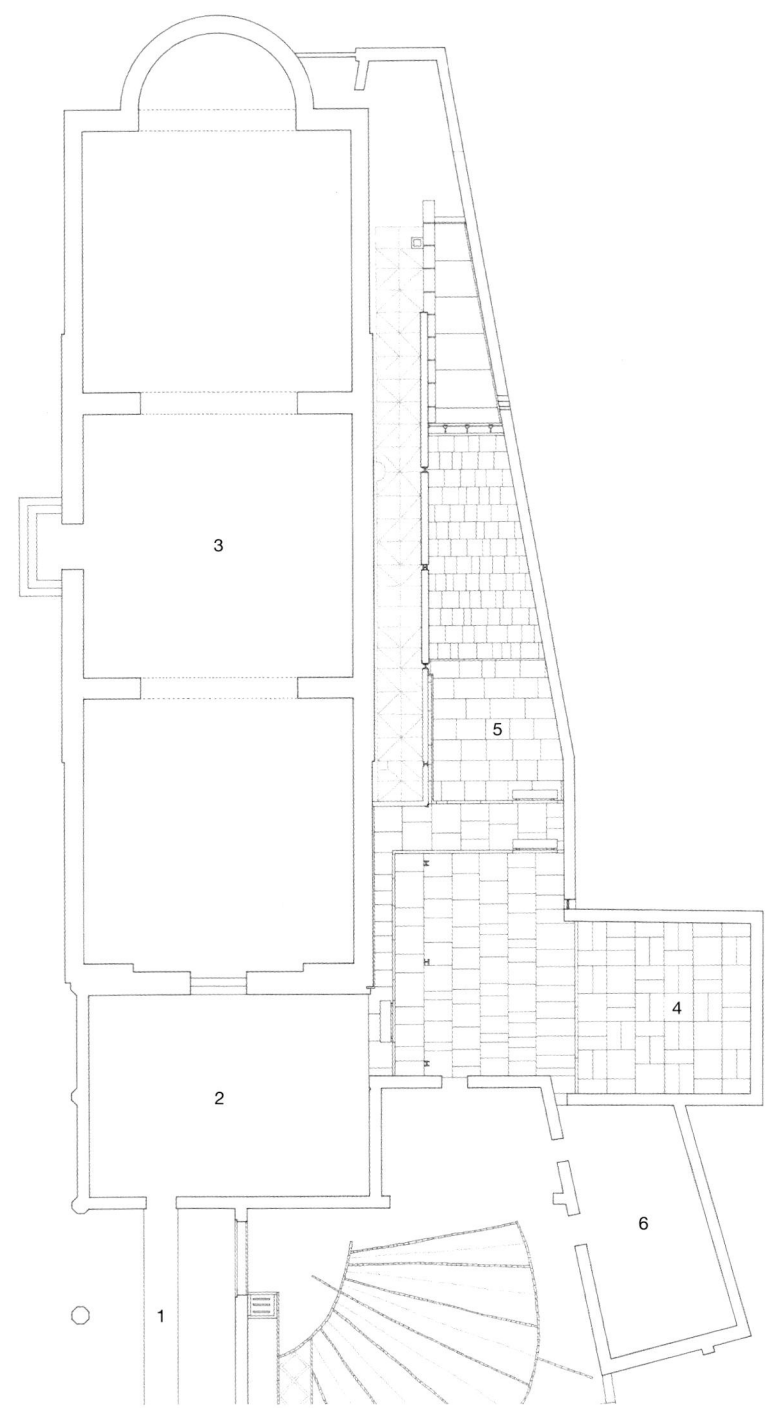

1. Floor plan. Key: 1 arcade, 2 entrance hall, 3 »Basilica«, 4 high gallery, 5 long gallery, 6 the former stables.
2. Reflected ceiling plan.

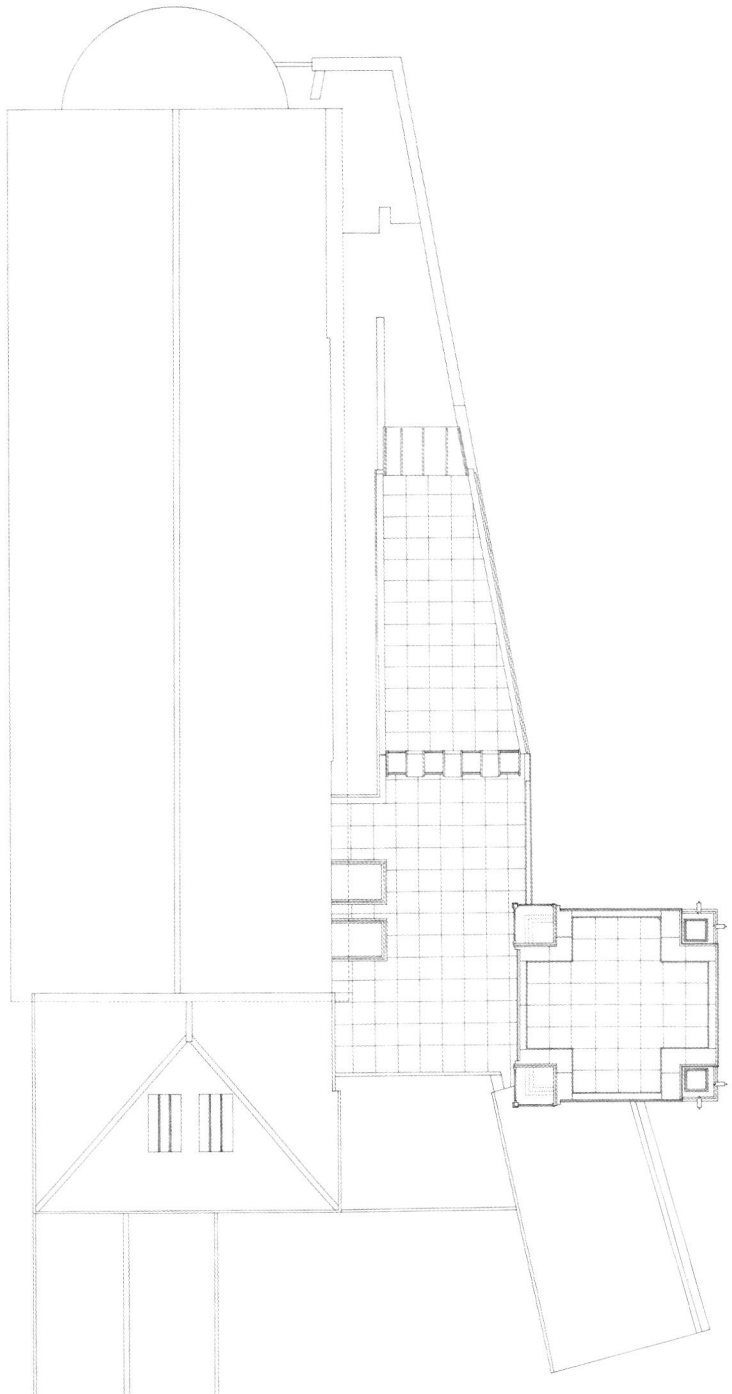

3–6. Cross sections.

7–10. Longitudinal sections.
(All plans by: Roger Thomson.)

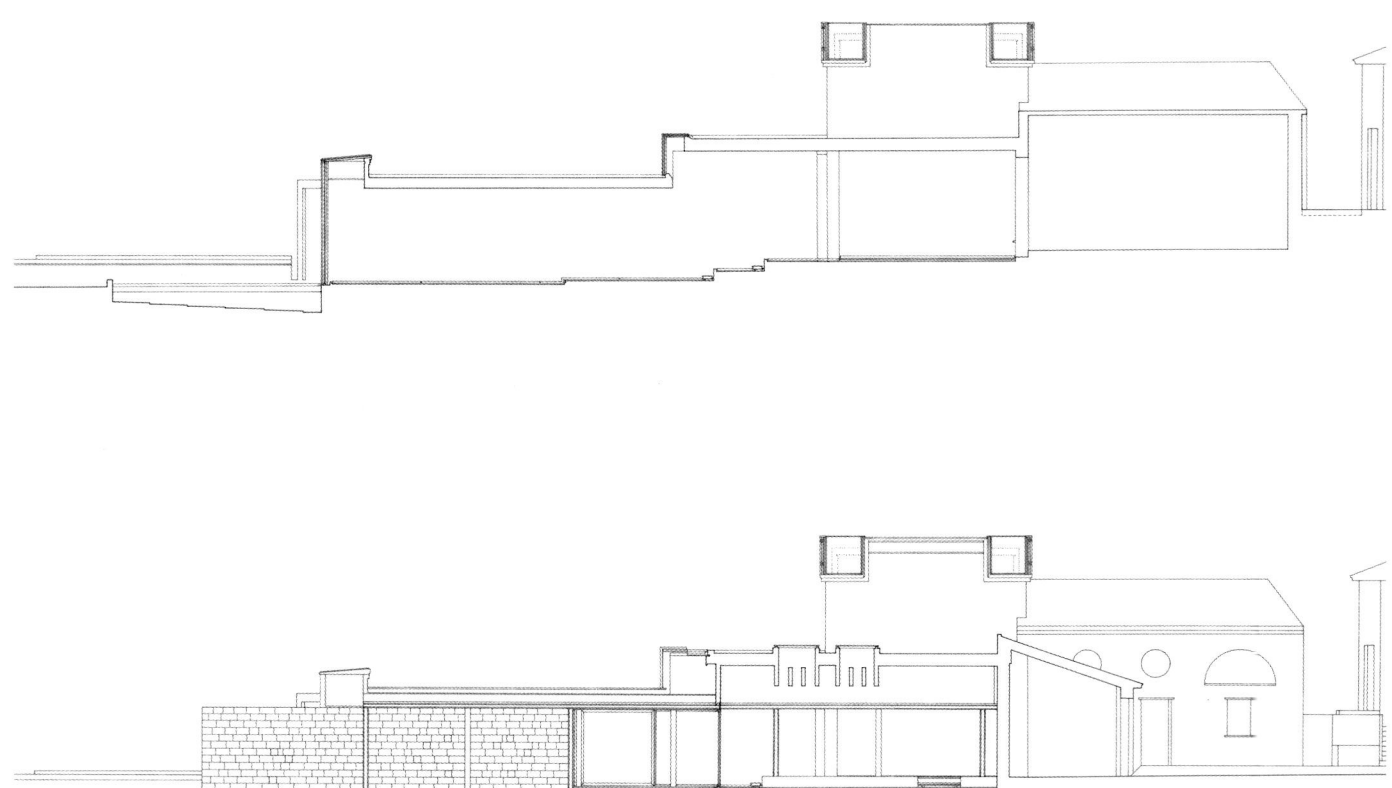

20

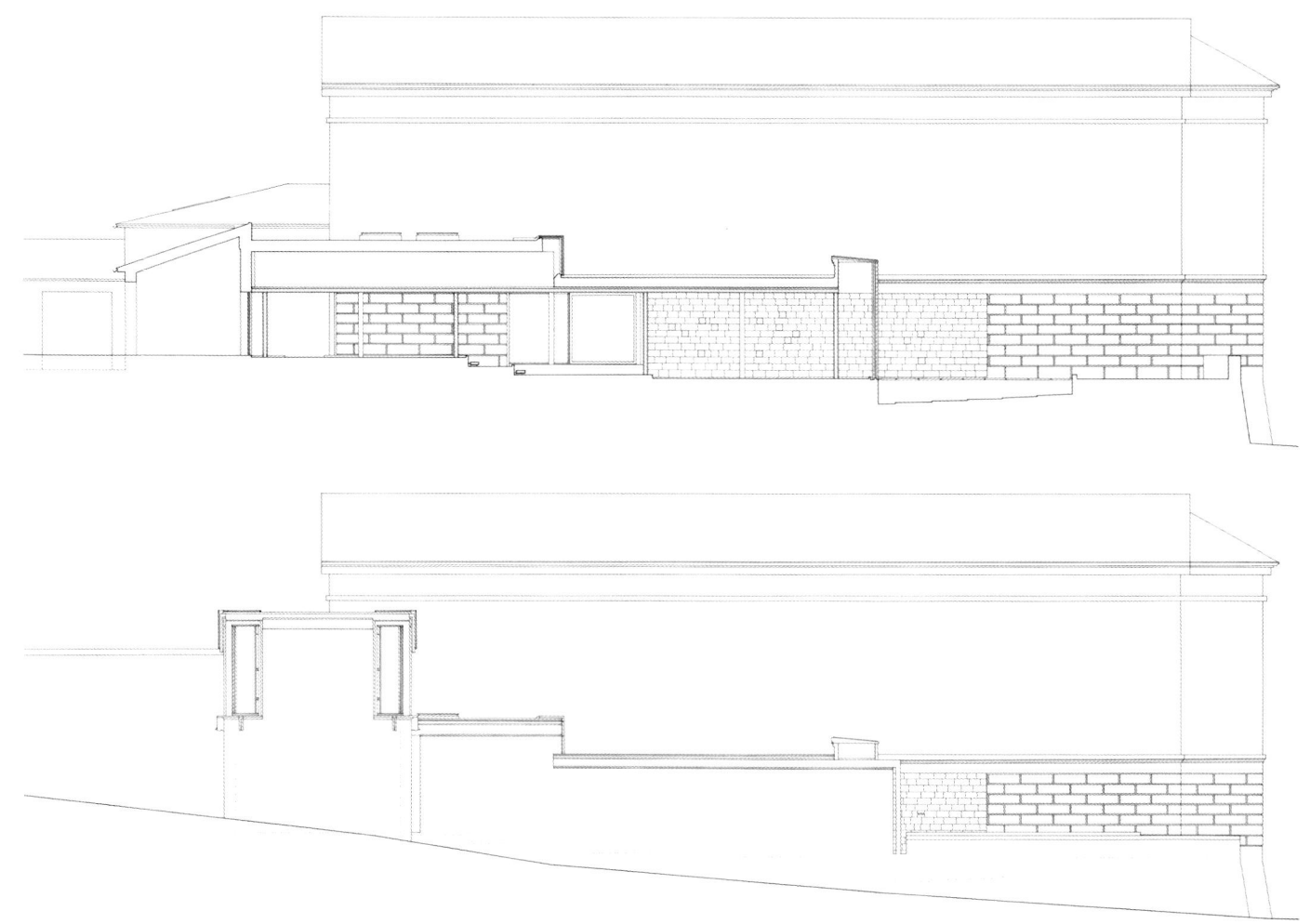

1. The entrance to the museum.
2. The arcade with the entrance to the »Basilica« and the Scarpa wing in the background.

3, 4. The entrance hall looking towards the »Basilica«.

5, 6. The »Basilica«.

7, 8. The entrance hall looking towards the Scarpa wing.

9, 10. The high gallery.

11, 12. Detailed views of the high gallery.

13. The four glass rectangles in the high gallery.
14. Detailed view of one of the glass rectangles.

p. 36/37
15. The long gallery. The high gallery is to the right.

p. 38, 39
16, 17. Detailed views of the long gallery looking towards its little garden

18, 19. Detailed views of the long gallery looking back towards the high gallery.

20. View from the high gallery towards the entrance hall.
21. Detailed view of the entrance to the Scarpa wing. The entrance hall is to the right.

p. 44, 45
22. The Scarpa wing looking towards the mountains.

p. 46, 47
23, 24. Detailed views of the Scarpa wing.

25. View over the roofs of the entrance hall and the arcade towards the high gallery with the pediment of the »Basilica« to the left.
26. Detailed view of one of the high gallery's cubic glass rectangles.

p. 50, 51
27. View of the high gallery with the former stables to the left.
28. Detailed view of one of the high gallery's tall glass rectangles.

29, 30. The courtyard in front of the former stables.

31, 32. The former stables, now a gallery, looking towards the Scarpa wing.

33. The garden with Canova's house to the right and the »Basilica« to the left.
34. View of Canova's house from the garden.

p. 58
35. The plaster-cast storeroom in Canova's house.

Kurt W. Forster
The museum as civic catalyst

Museums emerged as public institutions in the early nineteenth century. As long as only one wing of a noble residence, or even an entire building, was designated as a picture gallery, the museum in the modern sense of the term had not yet taken form, for only as an independent structure on a prominent urban site could it begin to play its role as cultural protagonist. Not unlike the grand theater buildings that preceded the museum, and the railroad stations that followed it, the first shrines of art made their appearance in a number of cities within an astonishingly short time. Karl Friedrich Schinkel's Altes Museum (1823 to 1830) in Berlin's Lustgarten combined an eminently educational purpose with a location in the privileged ambit of the royal palace. Its colonnaded facade and ample vestibule lured visitors from the Lustgarten, leading them through an elegant escalier royal toward an elevated balcony: from on high, framed by grand Ionic columns, a panoramic view of the city opened up before them, while, behind them, on the walls of the vestibule, the story of human civilization unfolded in a single sweep with a series of painted scenes.

With his programmatic siting of the museum, Schinkel brought a new bourgeois institution face to face with the royal palace, which in turn would face up to the new presence of the public within a domain previously reserved for the monarchy. Flanking the cathedral on the island of the Spree, and acting as a foil to the prospect from Unter den Linden, Schinkel's museum was ideally placed and designed to serve the purposes that the Berlin philosopher Georg Wilhelm Friedrich Hegel had attributed to the temple in Greek antiquity: »among these single and double colonnades that lead immediately into the open, we see the people move freely, in casual groups or alone ... In this way the impression of the temple is at once simple and grand, but also serene, open, and pleasant inasmuch as the entire building is apt to offer a place to stroll, to assemble, to come and go at will.«[1] No more effective site and no more compelling scheme could be imagined for the display of historic schools of painting in galleries and selected works of sculpture in the central rotunda. In this way, Schinkel brilliantly inaugurated the dual purpose of modern museums by creating a grand public effect upon the city on the one hand, and offering a point of observation from which the cityscape assumed a new coherence and significance on the other.

While the history of collecting is long and complicated, the museum is a relatively recent institution and yet it has already witnessed dramatic transformations.[2] Museums found their initial identity in the royal treasure house and the private cabinet of curiosities. They gradually expanded to accommodate ever larger accumulations of artifacts and increased public access through the nineteenth century; only recently have they assumed a much more spectacular role in cultural life.[3] What had been a place of contemplation, where rigorously selected works of art were held up to public admiration as models for aesthetic judgment, in due course began to welcome the likes of photography, cinema, and video to its collections, but above all, museums adopted the idea of performance as a way of overcoming their past identity as dusty repositories.

In the twentieth century, a new kind of exhibition inspired by the experience of temporary exhibitions at the world's fairs of the nineteenth century came into

1. Karl Friedrich Schinkel, Altes Museum, Berlin, 1823 to 1830.
2. Renzo Piano and Richard Rogers, Centre national d'art et de culture Georges Pompidou (Beaubourg), Paris, 1971–77. (Photo: Richard Einzig.)
3. Hans Hollein, Guggenheim Museum Salzburg, 1989, project.

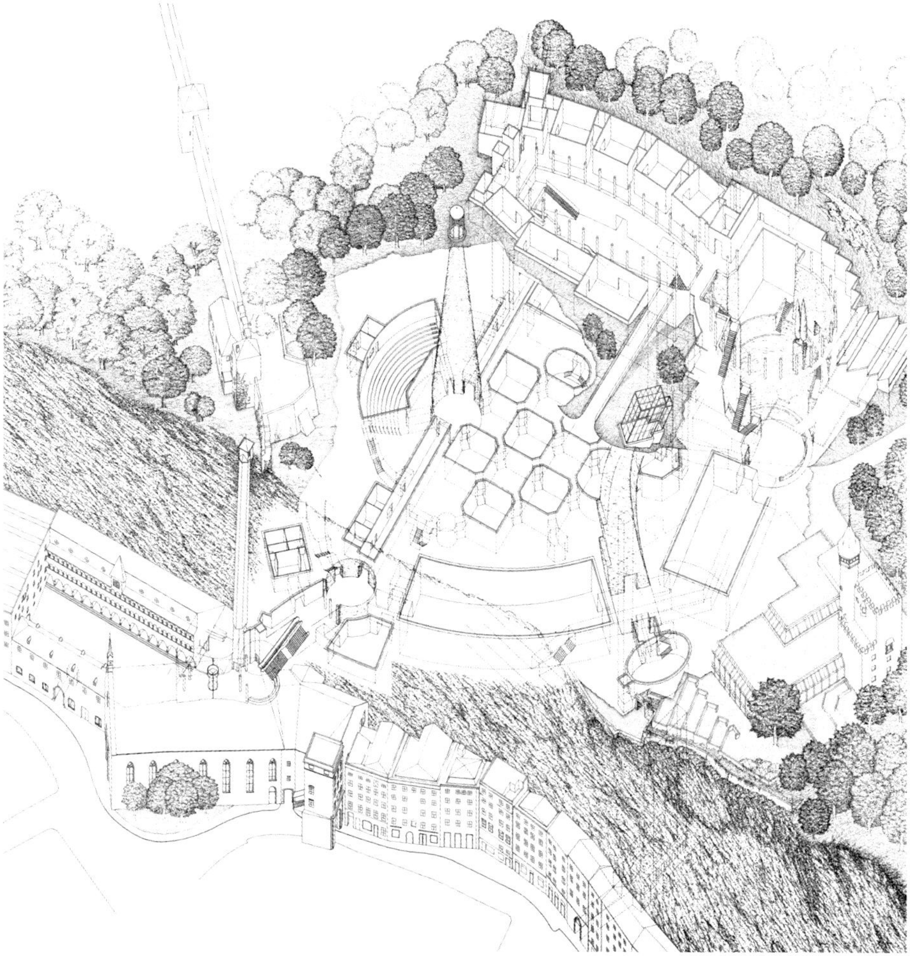

being. The »loan exhibition« burst onto the scene, stirring the public with its theatrical nature and its often nationalistic or otherwise partisan purposes. Although rare and ephemeral at first, loan exhibitions have completely transformed the modern museum and permanently altered the public's perception of art in general. Only a handful of museums remain aloof, refusing to lend works of art and abstaining from showing anything but their own permanent holdings, while the special exhibition has almost become the standard form by which museums keep rekindling the interest of their public. What has happened, in effect, amounts to a reversal of the museum's original purpose. No longer is its primary mission to uphold the exclusive value of highly select works of art; rather it propagates knowledge of many diverse and often competing – if not mutually exclusive – artistic practices. Such changes in their role did not leave the form of museum buildings unaffected. If museums were initially conceived to display finite bodies of individual works, they began to present ever larger masses of specialized artifacts, only to assume gradually an identity far closer to that of theaters. Today, museums have become venues for exhibitions of works from far and near, assembled according to ever different ideas and standards, and put on display for a short season or sent on tour to different cities.

The dramatic changes that have transformed the purposes of the museum did not entirely overwhelm its origins, but they have certainly changed the nature of its operations. The maintenance of permanent collections and the fairly frequent modification of their display remain central to many institutions, yet the presentation of a museum's traditional core collection has been deeply affected by recent events. The Guggenheim Museum in Bilbao extends this general development a step further: conceived to form a link in a possible chain of institutions under the aegis of the Guggenheim Museum in New York, Bilbao becomes the test site of an entirely novel museological concept. After Peggy Guggenheim's death, her private

museum in Venice reverted to the mother house in New York in 1976. Director Thomas Krens began to envision further expansion of its ambit to yet other cities: in 1989, he tested the waters in Salzburg, and, after Hans Hollein's operatic project for a museum hewn from a rocky cliff failed to materialize, Krens moved on to open a temporary branch of the Guggenheim in Berlin and laid the groundwork for an affiliated museum in Bilbao.

The »modern« idea of developing a chain of museums is both startling – when considered in light of the innate conservatism of museums – and disarmingly simple. If museums are indeed the unsuspecting heirs of the theater, then the idea of a chain of houses is only a logical consequence of their new condition. Instead of confining works of art to the place where they have found a permanent home, more often than not as a matter of accident rather than design, they would be periodically rotated, shown in changing assembly and under differing local conditions. Over time, the growing body of a set of collections would begin to form a larger pool of works than any single museum might ever hope to acquire for itself. The practice of loan exhibitions has not declined to the degree that was often prophesied, because modern methods of conservation and shipment manage to contain, to a degree, the negative effects traveling exhibitions can have on works of art, and, in any case, the ability to obtain loans depends as much on reciprocal lending as on the curatorial and logistical soundness of exhibition projects. Major loan exhibitions continue to be planned well into the next century, and the idea of linking up several museums on different continents for the purpose of endowing each one of them temporarily with works they could otherwise rarely – if ever – display may well be realistic. This new »franchising« of museum collections represents one response, and a precisely calibrated one at that, by which museums might react to the conditions that define their operation throughout the world.[4]

These expectations for the Guggenheim Museum in Bilbao surely played a role in its architectural conception. In 1991, Thomas Krens invited three architects to Bilbao, asking them to sketch out their ideas for a museum building in keeping with this novel pur-

4. Frank O. Gehry, Guggenheim Bilbao Museoa, 1991 to 1997. (Photo: Ralph Richter.)
5. Alvar Aalto, Essen Opera House, 1959–88.
6. Francesco Borromini, Collegio de Propaganda Fide, Rome, 1646–66. (Photo: Harry Seidler.)
7. Frank O. Gehry, Walt Disney Concert Hall, Los Angeles, 1988, project.

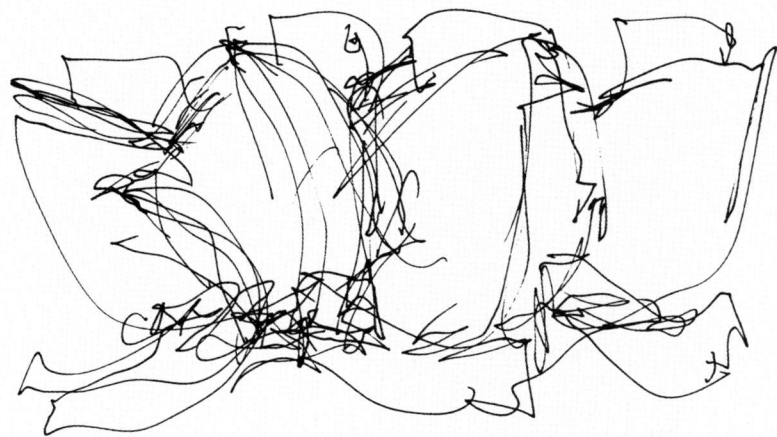

pose. Hans Hollein had already imagined a fantastic grotto carved from the Mönchsberg in Salzburg, and Arato Isozaki, another contender, already had several museums in Japan and the United States to his credit. Coop Himmelblau, the only match for Frank Gehry in terms of the theatricality of their previous projects, had built a pavilion for Alessandro Mendini's Museum in Groningen (1989/90), but they had not yet managed to secure a major commission for a metropolitan museum. Their experience with temporary installations and studio buildings for artists like Anselm Kiefer argued in their favor.

Thomas Krens's choice of architect was tempered by his previous experiences with museum projects and the ways their architects had of conceiving of them in terms of their recent typology and urban role. Almost two decades earlier, the opening of the Beaubourg museum in Paris marked the advent of museums that owe their identity less to permanent collections than to viceral impact.[5] Intended from the beginning as the venue for highly diverse events, the Beaubourg has lived up to its promise, and remains today the preferred exhibition site for visitors and Parisians alike. Never mind its obvious shortcomings – inadequate as the building may be for the display of paintings, unsound as it may be in its physical maintenance, and unsung as it is in the inconvenience it imposes on its staff – the Beaubourg fulfills the new museum's purposes above all by dint of its urban prominence. Comparable to an »aircraft-carrier of culture«, the Beaubourg berthed the idea of the »maison de la culture« in one of the neglected precincts of Paris, playing up its purpose as an attraction for the uninitiated as well as sophisticated elites. Just as Les Halles were once the place where the bourgeoisie went for oysters and champagne at midnight, the new cultural tourism now finds its mecca among collections dedicated to industrial design, film, video art, and a spectacular rooftop view of Paris thrown in for good measure. The Beaubourg's success is primarily one of urban function and cultural image, along the lines of the postwar Citroën and high-speed trains, and it also promised to vindicate French culture in the face of the worldwide expansion of the American avant-garde.

Ever since the Beaubourg opened in 1977, not only do new museum buildings need to stand the test as adequate repositories of art, but they are also expected to act as catalytic agents of urban transformation. These new museums help induce campaigns for the revitalization of derelict urban territory, as on the South Bank in London[6] or in the Amsterdam harbor, where Renzo Piano's new Metropolis Museum of Science opened in 1997. Already in 1988, with his winning entry in the competition for the Walt Disney Concert Hall in Los Angeles, Frank O. Gehry ushered in a decisive stage in the evolution of cultural buildings.

Two major art institutions herald equally definitive moments: Richard Meier's Getty Center in Los Angeles and Frank Gehry's Guggenheim Museum in Bilbao. In both instances, the architect was asked to conceive work on a scale and in a location that perilously challenged the limits of any living architect's ability. Significantly, the institutions behind these projects had thrived in the expansionist era of the 1980s, when art as enterprise and spectacle called for buildings that were so intensely of their moment that they were unlikely to have many successors.[7]

Gehry's project for the Walt Disney Concert Hall and the Museum in Bilbao are both located in what had become derelict urban zones, places scored by traffic and trade arteries, criss-crossed by major sight lines, but lacking in any clear manifestation of character. In Los Angeles, the concert hall was expected to serve as the centerpiece in a scheme to rebuild a

grand municipal complex of museums and hotels. These were envisioned in the midst of future corporate and private development. In Bilbao, where heavy industry and fluvial warehouses had long been abandoned, a swath of raw embankment along the Nervión River was slated for redevelopment. The latter site is not only cramped by rail and street corridors alongside the river, but also by its marginal location and an inclined suspension bridge that plunges from the east over steep river banks right into the ensanche. Between the bifurcating ramps of the bridge, the slope, and the river, a large irregular site was set aside for Gehry's project. The compromised conditions of the site make an apt metaphor for the complex circumstances under which the commission was precipitated by the regional and municipal governments in negotiations with the Guggenheim Museum in New York.[8]

Such grand projects as the Bilbao Guggenheim place extra burdens on the traditional institution of the museum. Museums increasingly find themselves implicated in a host of new and highly publicized activities, but they have also become the preferred sites of the bravura architectural performance, as, for example, with the extension planned for the Victoria and Albert Museum, and the new wing of the Berlin Museum by Daniel Libeskind.[9] As museums have been forced to find new ways of financing themselves, they resort to the kind of gambits with which Phineas Taylor Barnum filled his circus tents. The exaggeration of the public status of museums – not in all cases dependent on new buildings, though rarely accomplished without them – has also led to important changes in their architectural character. New museums require a grand and ever more impressive public presence, and equally inventive and varied interiors. The achievement of volumetric presence on the outside and a spatial expansiveness on the inside calls for dramatic transitions, even magical transport, of the vistor's experience.

In his late works, Alvar Aalto molded spatial relationships into a constantly varying continuum, as if space were able to break free of Cartesian abstraction and assume a viscous state. After the Second World War, Le Corbusier increasingly confronted the abstraction of »space« with the volumetric presence of bodily shapes, curving ramps, and shell-like alcoves. But the antinomy of body and cage, which he had put to analytic purpose in his paintings since the late 1920s, was progressively »resolved«, or rather suppressed, with the unchecked ascendancy of the cage over the body after Le Corbusier's death. As an abstraction reinforced by economic imperatives, the skeletal structure of buildings became so pervasive after the War as to make a virtual prisoner of the body. Not so for Alvar Aalto and Hans Scharoun, whose explorations left their mark on Gehry's thinking. Like Aalto, Gehry began early to mold volumes in fluid contours and sweeping curves; like Scharoun, he advanced more rapidly toward his goal in complex but flowing interiors, in which continuous rather than segmented deformations became the rule. As Gehry gained a new freedom in shaping surfaces, he moved beyond the stage of Aalto's Essen Opera House (1959 to 1988).

With his buildings of the 1980s, Frank Gehry returned to an architecture possessed of powerful corporeal qualities. He does not think of the volumes of his buildings within the confines of abstract space (which is also the space of economics); rather, he engages these volumes in intimate relationships with one another. In short, he sets the bodies of his buildings in motion as a choreographer does his or her dancers. One need only observe Gehry's manner of drawing to gain an immediate sense of his way of thinking: the pen does not so much glide across the page as it dances effortlessly through a continuum of space. Gehry's studio practice recalls nothing so much as performance rehearsals, days and weeks of choreographic invention and refinement that requires all dancers to be present all of the time. The architect's affinity for the transitory and his conjurer's grasp of minute displacements are fueled by his knowledge of performance art and enriched by his collaborations with artists. For years now, his friendship with Claes Oldenburg has moved well beyond occasional collaboration – as in the Chiat-Day-Mojo Building in Venice, California (1986–91) – toward a give-and-take that only artists with a keen sense for both collective performance and individual invention are able to develop.

At Bilbao, Gehry has been planning with and for artists, providing spaces for specially commissioned installations as well as flexible galleries for the inevitable variety of exhibition displays. The building complex includes generously proportioned areas for public events and unforeseen opportunities that vastly expand the purposes of contemporary museums.[10] It is entirely purposeful that the museum has been anchored in the cityscape of Bilbao like a vast circus tent surrounded by a congerie of caravans, for the variety of events anticipated to take place there requires large and ever varying venues. Subsidiary spaces are clustered together, squeezed through the bottleneck between river and embankment, made to duck under bridges, and finally allowed to soar over the building's core in a spectacular canopy. All this implies motion induced by internal tension and external compression and gives rise to the towering and seemingly revolving space of the central hall. If it is possible to speak of a spatial realm that lacks figural contours yet possesses powerful bodily qualities, if ambulation can unlock the complexities of a building's order beyond the outlines of the plan, then the Museum in Bilbao reawakens an architecture that has lain dormant for centuries. The suggestion may sound extravagant, but the reality of this building, which has been fashioned from segmented shells, surely bears it out. If one examines historic architecture in search of buildings that might presage what Frank O. Gehry has been able to achieve, one is likely to pay attention to Francescsco Borromini. One will do so not only because some of the same terms come to mind as one describes the salient traits of Borromini's and Gehry's buildings, terms such as »undulation« and »undulating and zigzagging forms«.[11] Whatever the critical suppositions may be, the terms that get affixed to an architecture that so clearly defies both the traditional nomenclature of its parts and the experiential categories of its impact, is bound to meet as much criticism as acclaim. Because the sheer effect of the Bilbao Guggenheim overwhelms and continues to intrigue, is not unlike the fascination Borromini's buildings held for his fellow architects and even his sometime-employer

Notes

[1] Georg Wilhelm Friedrich Hegel, Werke, ed. by E. Moldenhauer and K. M. Michel, Frankfurt a. M., 1986, XIV, p. 320. Hegel repeated his »Vorlesungen über die Ästhetik«, from which this passage is taken, throughout the 1820s, and Wilhelm von Humboldt and Johann Wolfgang von Goethe were sanguine in their approval of Schinkel's plans for the Museum. See also: Walter Hochreiter, Vom Musentempel zum Lernert. Zur Sozialgeschichte deutscher Museen 1800–1914, Darmstadt, 1994, esp. pp. 9–57.
[2] Compare: Krisztof Pomian, Der Ursprung des Museums, Berlin, 1988; Horst Bredekamp, Die Geschichte der Kunstkammer und die Zukunft der Kunstgeschichte, Berlin, 1993; Ekkehard Mai, Expositionen. Geschichte und Kritik des Ausstellungswesens, Munich and Berlin, 1986.
[3] See: Kurt W. Forster, »Shrine? Emporium? Theater? Two Decades of American Museum Building«, Zodiac, 6 (1991), pp. 30–75.
[4] The following offer useful surveys: Heinrich Klotz and Waltraud Krase, New Museum Buildings in the Federal Republic of Germany, Frankfurt a. M. and Munich, 1985; Josep M. Montaner, Museums for the New Century, Barcelona, 1995; »Contemporary Museums« Architectural Design, London, 1997.
[5] See: Nathan Silver, The Making of Beaubourg: A Building Biography of the Centre Pompidou, Paris, Cambridge, MA, 1994.
[6] In 1996, Richard Rogers won a competition to renovate the South Bank area altogether. He proposed a huge canopy under whose undulating, glass-clad roof the existing buildings, such as the rather coarse Hayward Gallery, assume the appearance of architectural cliffs washed by the gentler waves of a new era of elegance and luxury.
[7] Kurt W. Forster, »A Citadel for Los Angeles and an Alhambra for the Arts«, a+u. Architecture and Urbanism, 11, 1992, pp. 6–15. Compare Meier's own account of his experiences: Richard Meier, Building the Getty, New York, 1997.
[8] The evolution of the Museum in Bilbao has been chronicled by Coosje van Bruggen in her book Frank O. Gehry: Guggenheim Museum Bilbao, New York, 1998.
[9] See: Kurt W. Forster, »Monstrum mirabile et audax«, in: Daniel Libeskind. Extension to the Berlin Museum with Jewish Museum Department, exhibition catalogue, Berlin, 1992, pp. 17–23. Another museum by Libeskind, the Nussbaum Museum in Osnabrück, is currently under construction.
[10] See note 3.
[11] Francesco Milizia, Memorie degli architetti antichi e moderni, Bassano, 1785, 4th ed., II, p. 159 passim. It will be remembered that Milizia so characterized Borromini's work in order to decry it and warn architects and patrons of its corrosive effect on good taste – an altogether familiar litany also echoing from contemporary criticism of Gehry.
[12] Critique often cuts closer to the nature of certain phenomena than praise, and Bernini's somewhat envious description of Borromini's way of invention is very much to the point when he characterized Borromini's methodical search as »dentro una cosa cavare un'altra, e nel altra l'altra, senza finire mai.« For a more detailed comparison of Borromini's and Gehry's method of evolving ar-

chitectural forms, see the forthcoming monograph on Gehry: Francesco Dal Co and Kurt W. Forster, eds., *Frank O. Gehry*, New York, 1998. Cf. also: Christof Thoenes, »Die Formen sind in Bewegung geraten – Form has been set in motion«, *Daidalos*, 67 (1998), pp. 63–73.

[13] For this and other experiences, see the forthcoming publication: Kurt W. Forster, ed.: *Gehry in Conversation*, Stuttgart, 1998.

[14] Hal Iyengar, Larry Novak, Robert Sinn and John Zils, »The Guggenheim Museum, Bilbao, Spain«, *Structural Engineering International*, 1996, pp. 227–229.

Bernini[12], the phenomenon of its excessive nature deserves some consideration.

Explanations can frame Frank Gehry's design of the Guggenheim Museum in Bilbao within the recent design of museum buildings and trace its extraordinary emergence from his earlier – if unbuilt – projects like the Disney Concert Hall. What cannot be easily explained, much less argued into existence, is the sheer exhilaration that this building gives off, the jubilant excess of its presence. Before it can be considered anything else, the Bilbao Guggenheim must be reckoned overweight, overdone, and overwhelming. Its excessive qualities are precisely those that enable it to assume several different roles at once. It is an immovable pile in the city and a sinuous creature draping its body along a narrow ledge above the river. As a luminous cave on the inside, and a metallic mountain from without, the museum appears to be both a perfect fit and a perfect stranger in its site. Excess designates the state of the building, exuberance its true nature.

As with any other building, there is a history to this project that brings together the many strands of its real and imaginary origins, but there is also a paleo-history to it, a tale that precedes its own story. The events surrounding Gehry's project for the Disney Hall in Los Angeles mark a period in the architect's life that can be compared to an area of chilled volcanic rock. Destructive and barren at first, it later turns into fertile ground, laden with minerals that give it new life. In evolving the project for the Disney Concert Hall, Gehry turned his »winning ticket« into a license to embark on a voyage into the unknown. From his bold but still beholden entry into the competition, he went on to reshape all of its parts and mold them into a huge new creature of a building. The project ceased to resemble a group of distinctive characters, as he had cast them in several of his earlier projects, turning instead into a single, multiform, and many-limbed entity. The wonderment with which Gehry describes the many-armed Shiva he first saw in the collection of Norton Simon invokes the ideal of animation he sought to achieve for himself.[13] The project for the Concert Hall that he exhibited at the Venice Biennale in 1991 had just begun to run into serious trouble at home when instead a new prospect dawned over Bilbao.

The vigor and resolve with which Gehry attacked the Bilbao project sprang, initially and violently, from his disappointment over the Concert Hall. He had been passed over so many times for significant jobs in Los Angeles that he almost turned into his own best excuse for yet another defeat. When the Disney project fell to him, it afforded Gehry a release of extraordinary effect. In the space of less than two years, he transformed his improvisational method of working with rickety models of paper, plastic, wood, and sticks into a highly sophisticated process. For a number of years, he had been manipulating his models, bending and locking their walls, cutting and pasting their parts, but now he began to shape them into ever more fluid forms. He could only hope of turning these curvilinear shapes into actual buildings if the process by which they were invented could also be applied to the method of producing them. Gehry learned to transfer plastic shapes to and from the screen. Again, the Concert Hall had been the test case, and its limestone walls the demonstration piece for a stone-cutting process also governed by computer. Almost within the space of a single project, Gehry managed to take his intuitive approach to a level of technical definition that brought such idiosyncratic buildings within economic reach.

When it became clear that years might pass before the concert hall would be built, Gehry was saved from an all-too-familiar decline into resentment by the even more challenging opportunity in Bilbao. Instead of trimming his sails, he plowed straight into the wind and imagined a building more adventurous, grander, and more profligate than even the Disney Concert Hall. Perhaps inspired by a reckless kind of courage, he decided to carry on where he had been forced to lay off, rather than begin again at the beginning, as it were. From the very start, the sketches for Bilbao seemed to have a capacity to soar. They expanded energy as if it were free, and this freedom not only generated forms previously thought to be impossible, but also unfit for integration into a complicated site.

If one were to seek a single index for the historical standing of this building, one need only consider the novel applications of computer technology in its making. For the Bilbao Museum, Gehry tapped the full capacity of computer-assisted design. Leaving its auxiliary role far behind, he and his collaborators made use of programs that were originally developed for the design of airplane fuselages, but which in this case provided the matrix for the shaping of every part and the refinement of every element in the design and construction of the museum. The age-old distinction between the hands that design and the instruments that execute has been overcome: the separate phases and techniques of conceiving and executing a building here were woven into an unbroken »loop«. Every volume has been shaped in three dimensions, tested and modified by computer plotting, just as every part of its physical assembly – steel frame, cladding, and all – was fabricated on the basis of computer-generated construction documents.[14] Only in this way can the inaccurate fit among the conventionally separate phases of invention, transcription, and execution be perfected, and the exponential degree of geometric complexity of such a structure be realized without costly trial and error.

Not only will the Bilbao Museum go down as one of the most complex formal inventions of our time, but it will also stand as a monument to the productive capacities that are now at our disposal, insofar as an architect like Gehry pushes them to new heights of imaginative use. When complexities of an order commensurate with our understanding of the world can be restored to architecture, we shall no longer have to be content with the subsistence diet dictated by economics any more than with the impoverished aesthetics of an earlier era.

The Museum in Bilbao is a building that elicits superlatives: beginning with its immense scale and intricately ramified setting, and ending with one of the most complex spatial experiences to be had anywhere, its architectural qualities are virtually unique in our time.

1, 2. Floor plans (1st floor, 2nd floor).

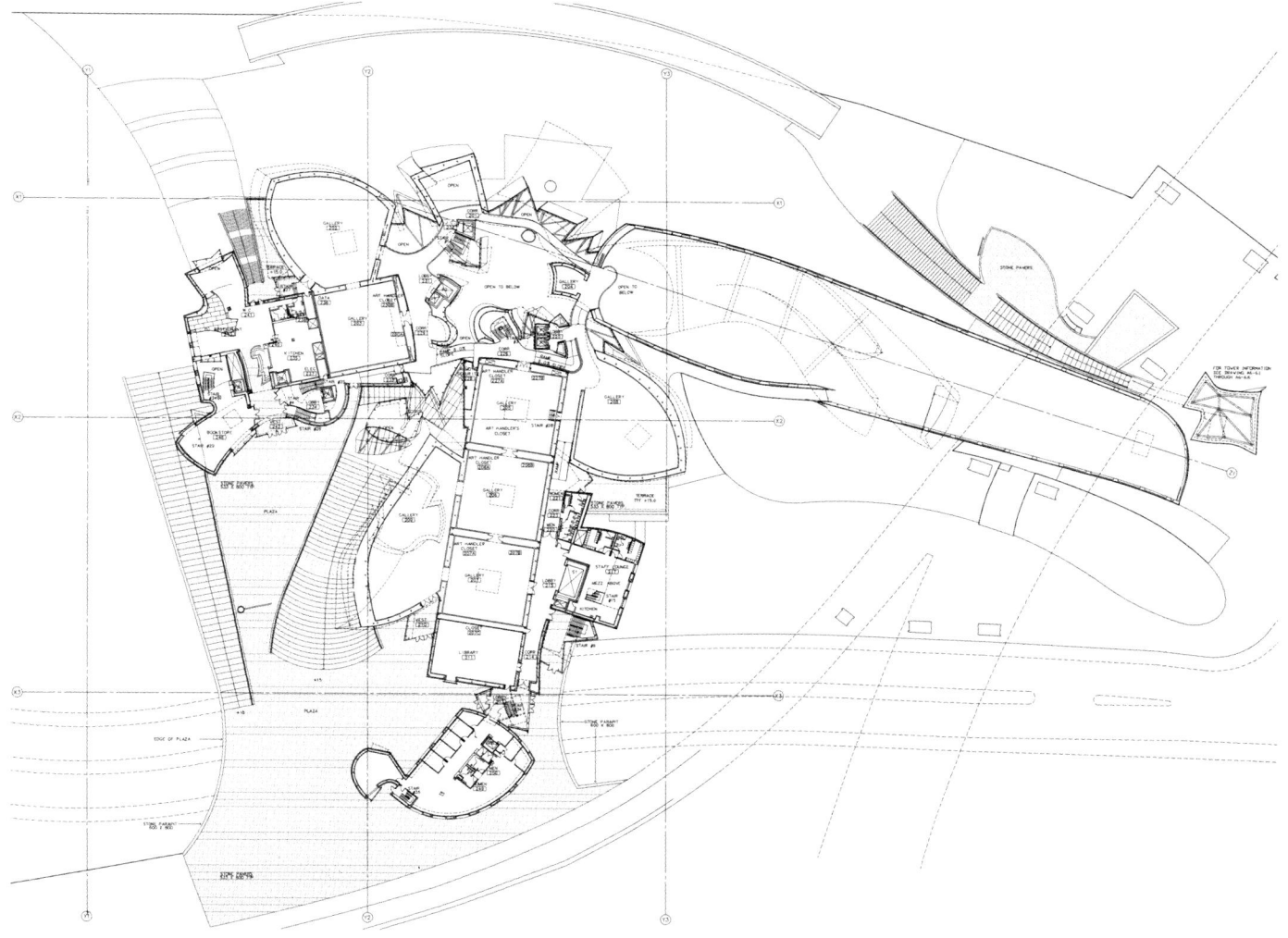

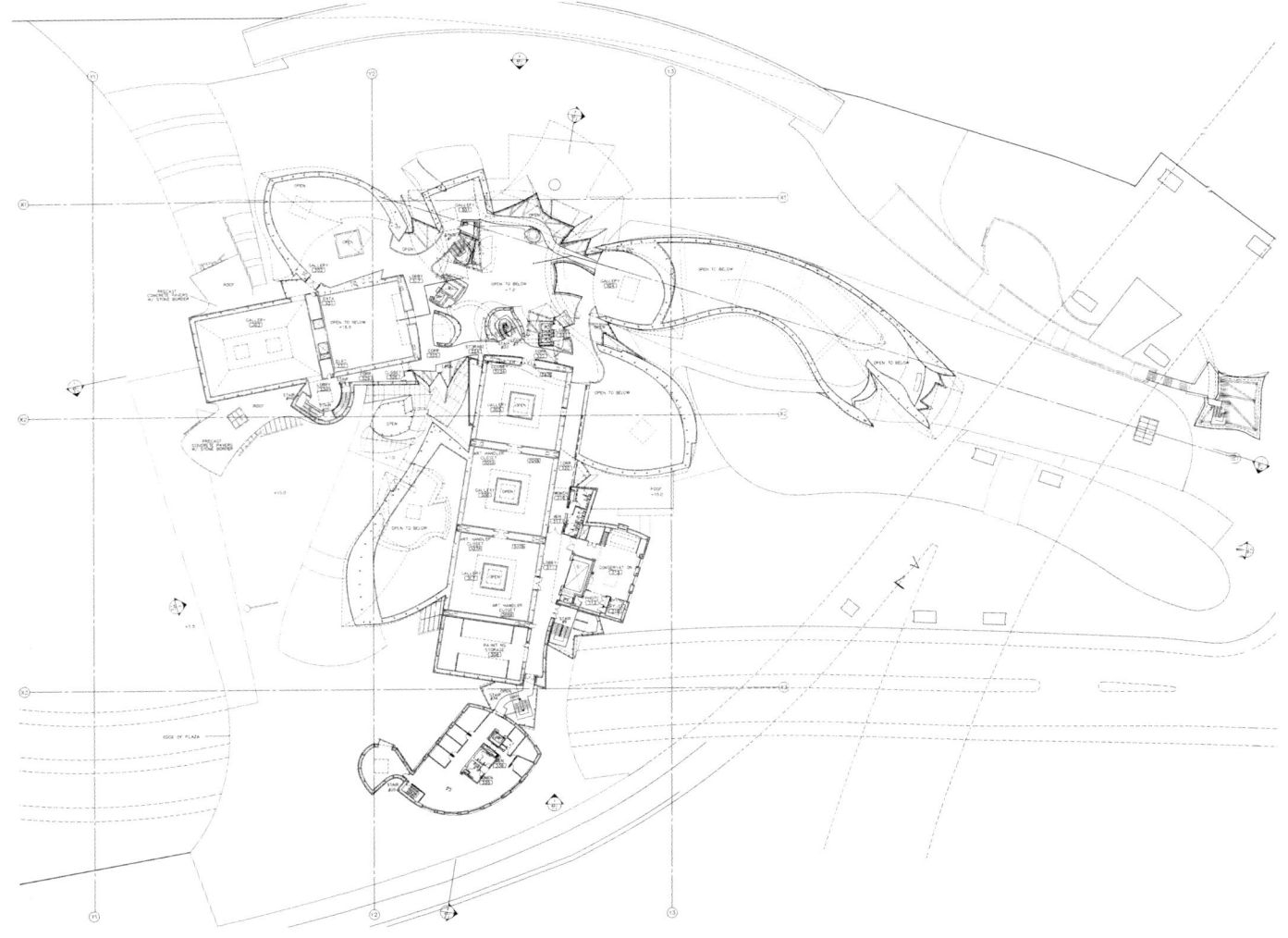

3, 4. Floor plans (3rd floor, 4th floor).

p. 70/71
5. Partial floor plan (3rd floor).

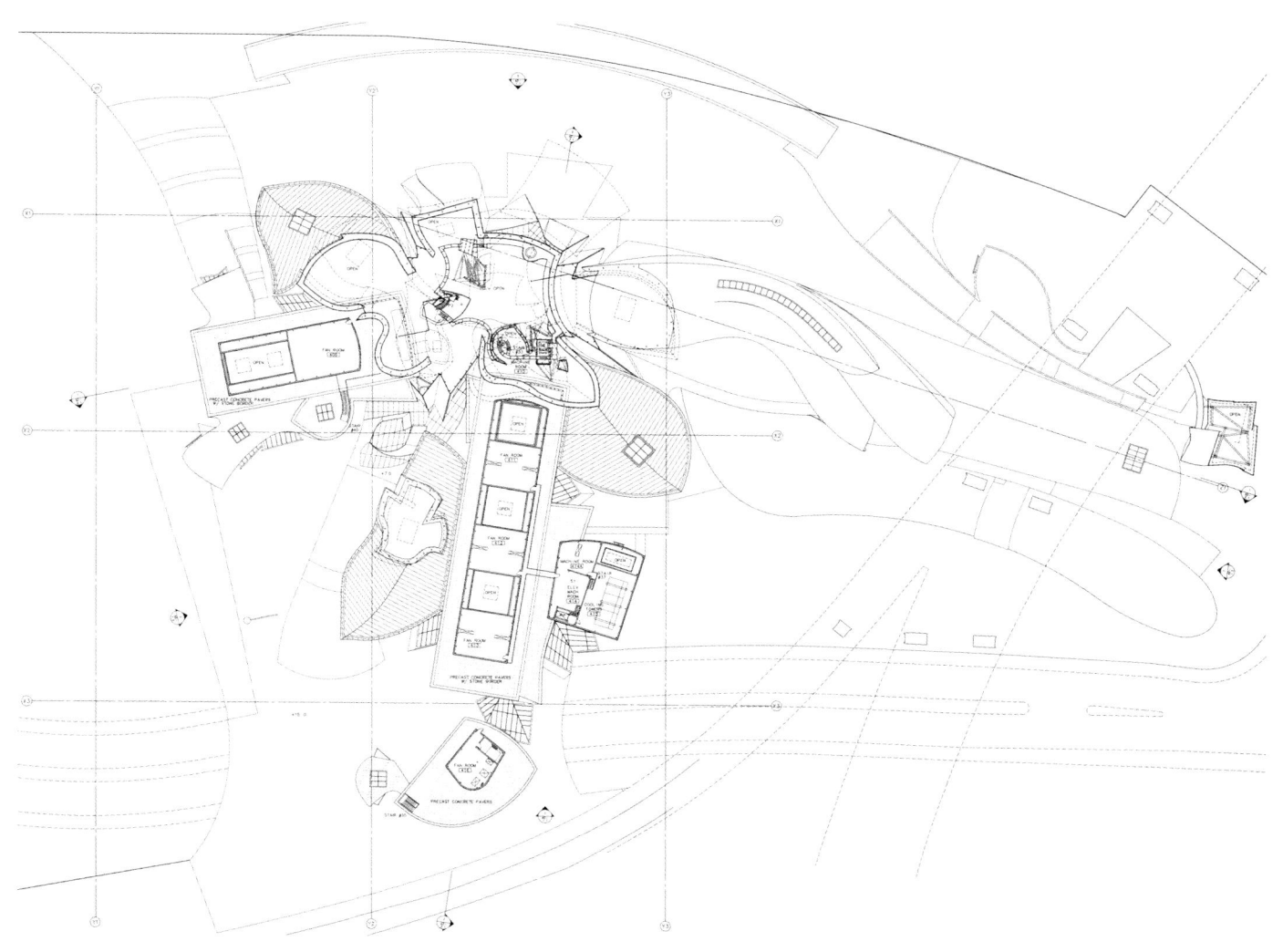

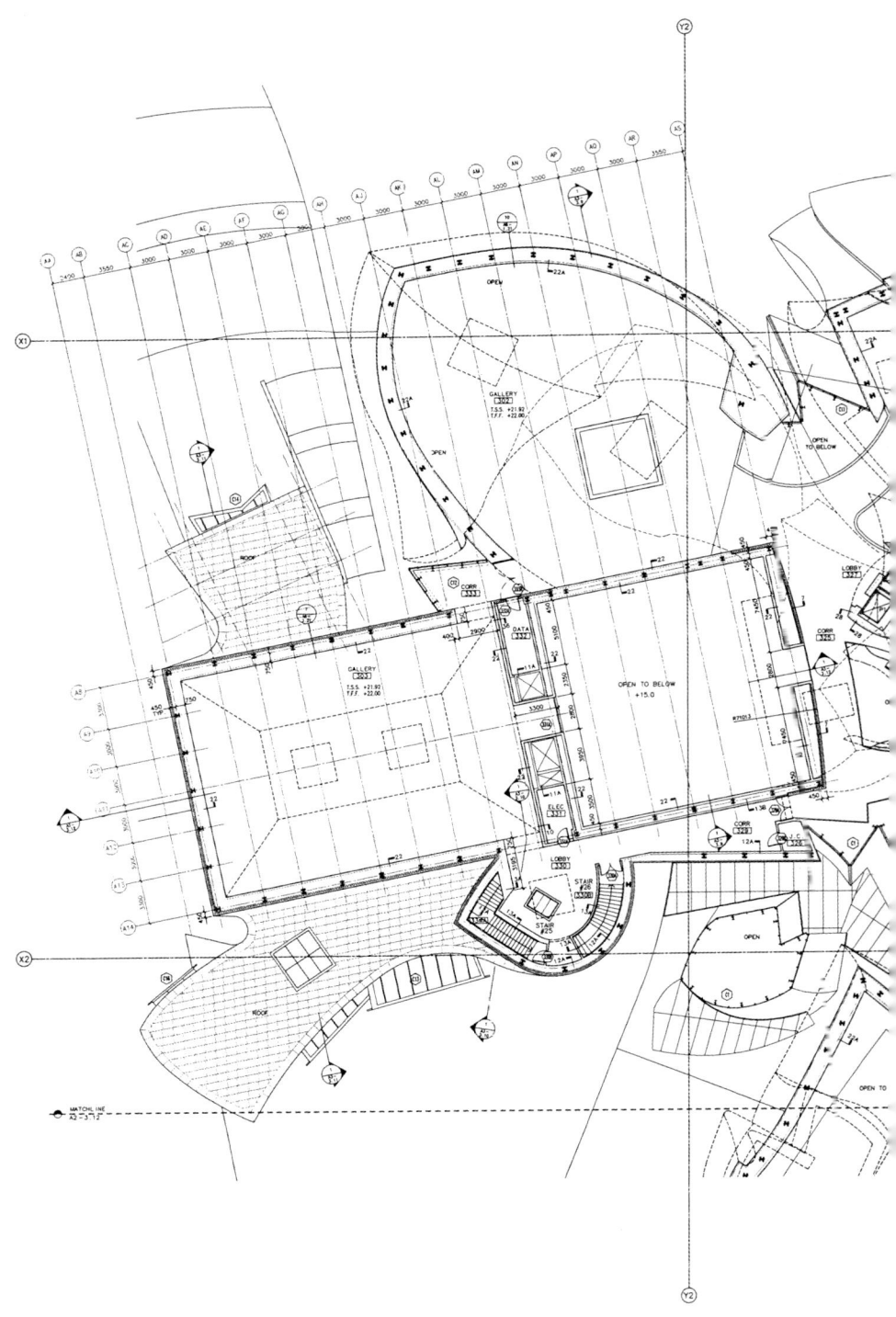

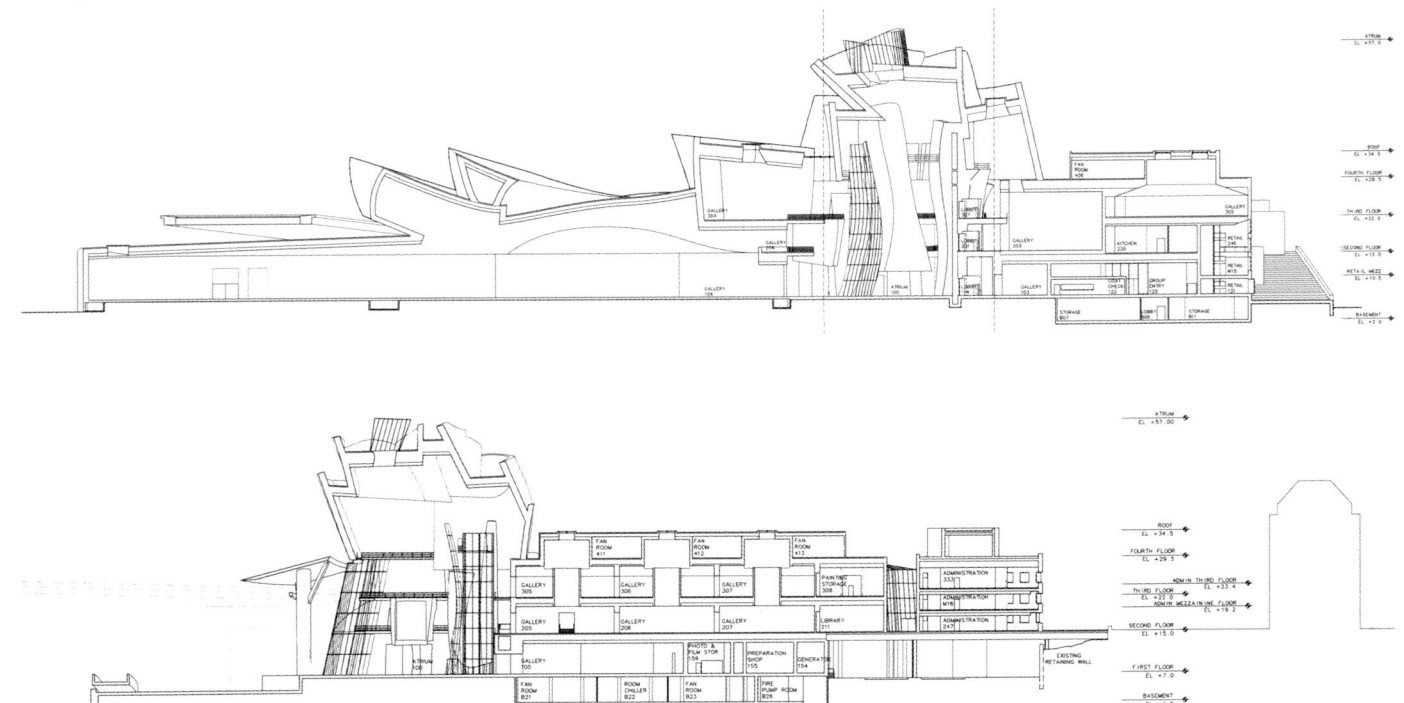

6–9. Sections.

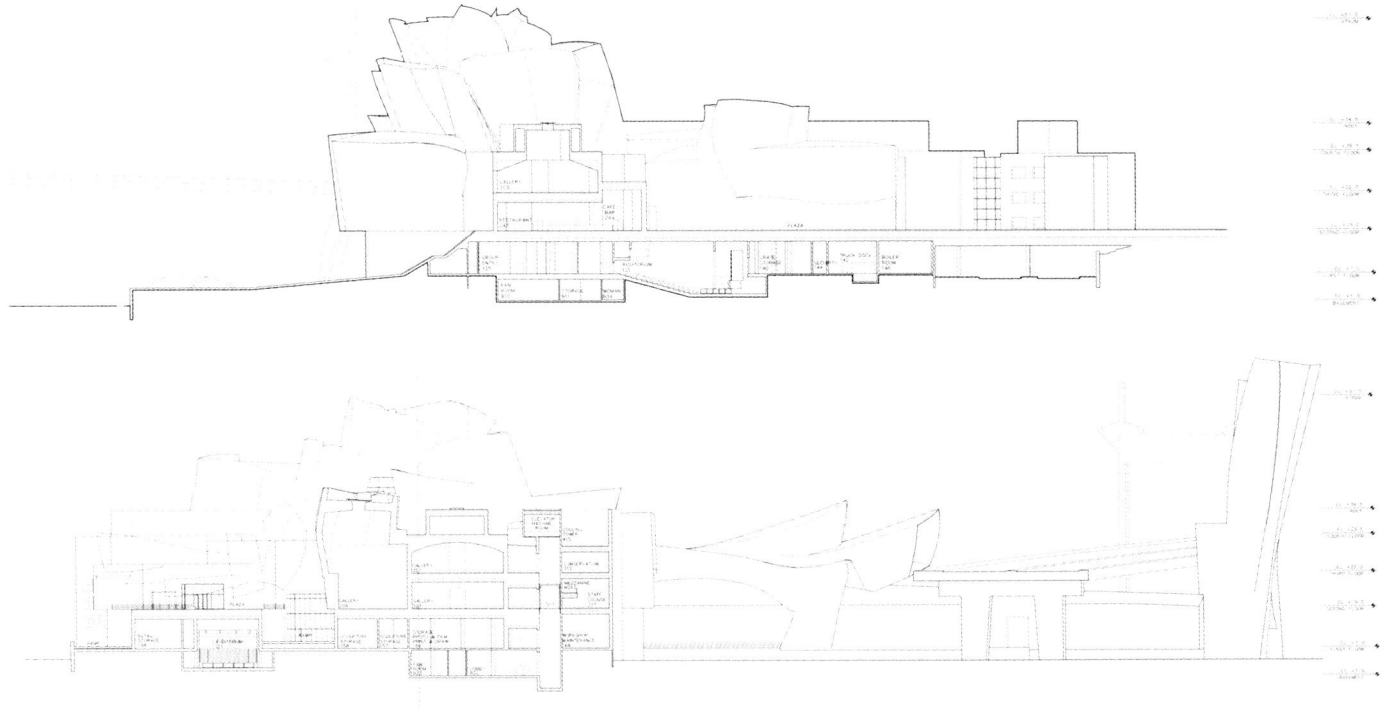

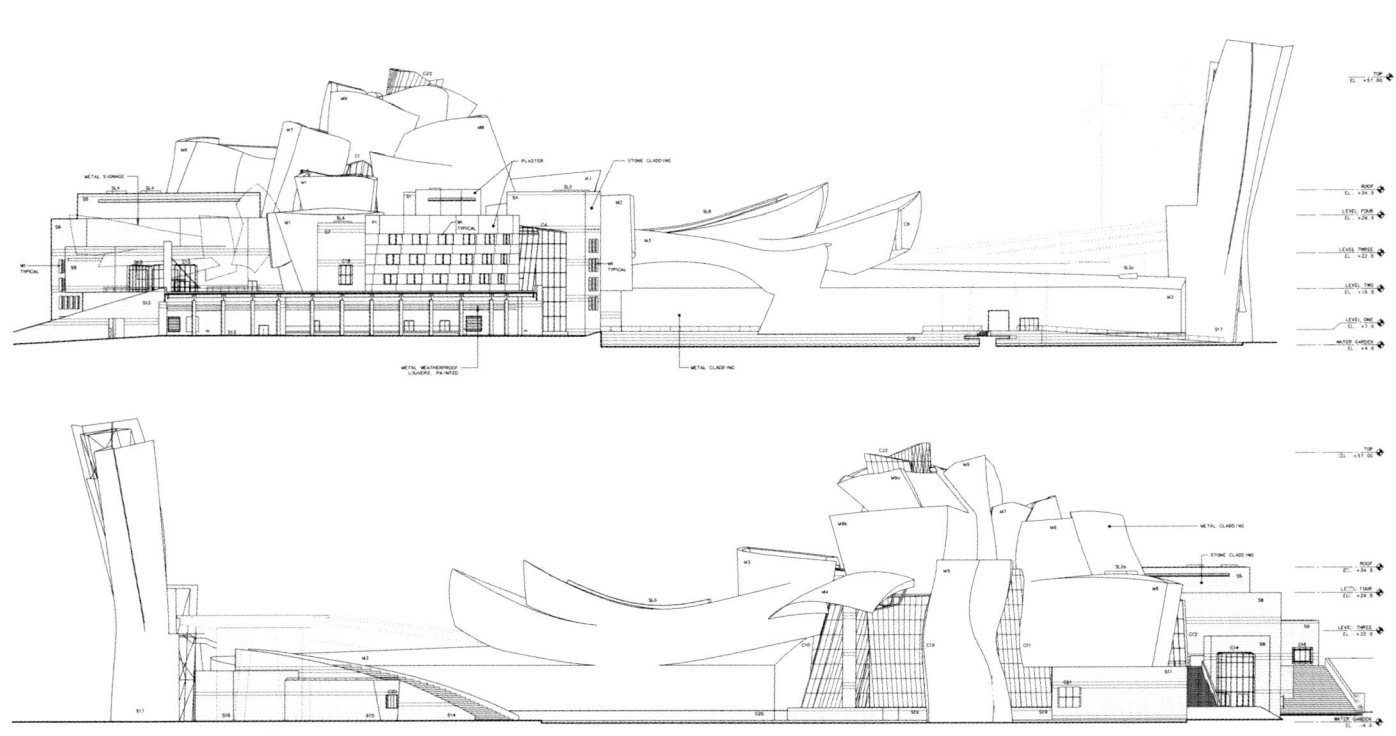

10. South elevation.
11. North elevation.
12. East elevation.
13. West elevation.

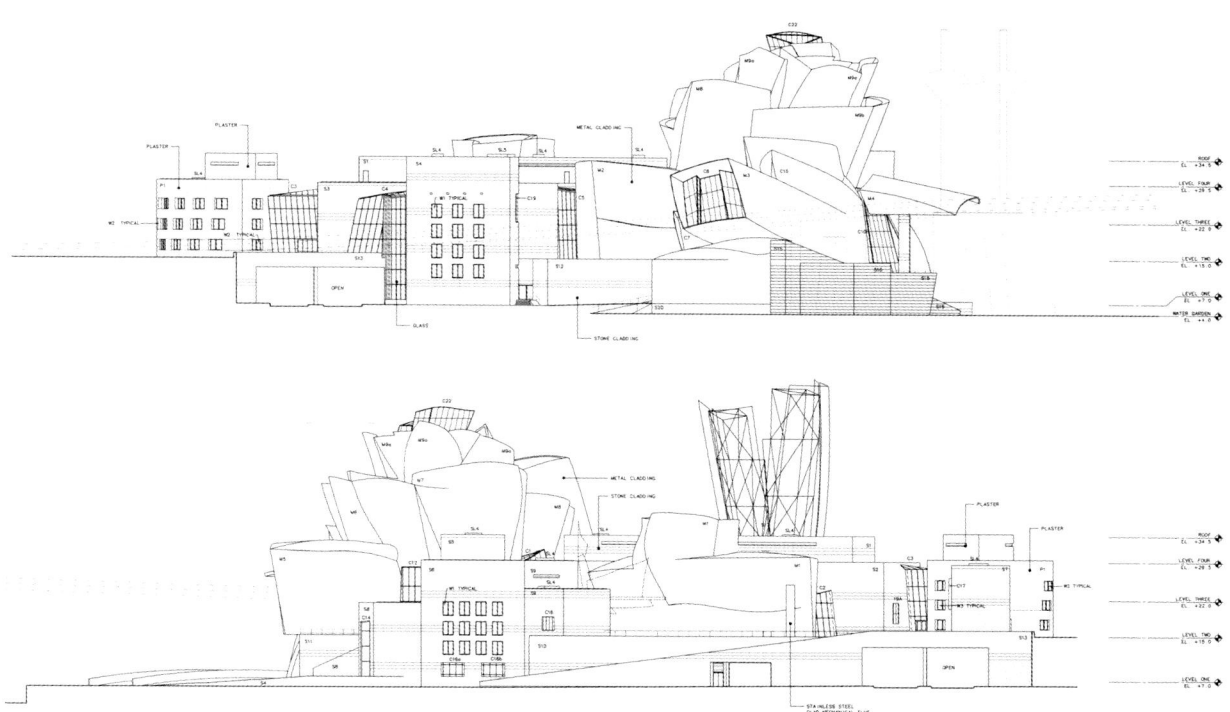

p. 76/77
1. General view from the northeast in the evening.

2. General view from the northeast.
3. General view from the northwest.
4. General view from the northeast with the nearby Puente de la Salve passing in the foreground.

5. The building seen from the south along Calle de Iparragguirre.
6. The building seen from the southeast with the tower situated east of the Puente de la Salve in the foreground.

7. Detail view from the west.
8. Detail view from the south with the east gallery in the background.
9. Detail view from the west with the east gallery on the right.

10. Detail view from the northeast with the glass wall of the atrium looking towards the Río de Nervión.
11. Detail view from the northwest with the glass wall of the atrium looking towards the Río de Nervión.

12–14. Detail views of the titanium cladding.

p. 88/89
15. Detail view from the east with the two glass openings of the upper part of the east gallery in the foreground.

16. Detail view from the east.
17. Detail view from the southwest, from the part on top of the main entry.

18, 19. Detail views from the southwest with the main entry.

p. 94, 95
20. The atrium looking north.
21. The atrium looking east with sculpture by Claes Oldenburg and Coosje van Bruggen.

p. 96, 97
22. The atrium looking southeast.
23. The atrium looking southwest.

p. 98, 99
24. The atrium looking northeast.
25. The atrium looking south.

26. The north section of the atrium looking east with sculpture by Claes Oldenburg and Coosje van Bruggen.
27. The north section of the atrium looking west.

p. 102/103
28. The atrium looking into the sky.

29, 30. Exhibition room in the south gallery with painting by Wassily Kandinsky and sculpture by Aristide Maillol.

31, 32. The east gallery looking west and east with sculpture by Richard Serra (© TAMCB Guggenheim Bilbao Museo,1998) and wall painting by Lawrence Weiner.

p. 108/109
33. General view from the northwest.

Guggenheim Bilbao Museoa
Abandoibarra Etorbidea, 2
Bilbao

Client
Guggenheim Bilbao Museoaren Fundazioa, Bilbao

Architects
Frank O. Gehry & Associates, Santa Monica, CA
Design director: Frank O. Gehry; project director: Randy Jefferson; project manager: Vano Haritunians; project architect: Douglas Hanson; project designer: Edwin Chan
Design team: Bob Hale, Rich Barrett, Karl Blette, Tomaso Bradshaw, Matt Fineout, David Hardie, Michael Hootman, Grzegorz Kosmal, Naomi Langer, Mehran Mashayekh, Chris Mercier, Brent Miller, David Reddy, Marc Salette, Bruce Shepard, Rick Smith, Eva Sobesky, Derek Soltes, Todd Spiegel, Jeff Wauer, Kristin Woehl

Structural engineers
Skidmore, Owings & Merrill, Chicago, IL
Senior structural consultant: Hal Iyangar; associate partner: John Zils; project engineer: Bob Sinn

Mechanical engineers
Cosentini Associates, New York, NY
Partner in charge: Marvin Mass; project engineer: Igor Bienstock; plumbing and fire protection: Tony Cirilo; electrical engineer: Edward Martinez

Acoustics and audiovision
McKay, Conant, Brook, Inc., Los Angeles, CA

Lighting design
Lam Partners, Boston, MA

Theater technology
Peter George Associates, New York, NY

Curtain wall
Peter Muller Inc., Houston, TX

Executive architects and engineers
IDOM, Bilbao
Project director: José Maria Asumendi; project manager: Luis Rodriguez Llopis; senior architect: César Caicoya

Martha Thorne
Reading between the lines: the museums of Rafael Moneo

Although one can argue that the practice of collecting art dates back many centuries, the first examples of buildings designed to display art collections publicly are relatively recent creations. Tracing the roots of the present-day museum to the eighteenth century immediately reveals two icons: the British Museum, which opened its doors in 1759, and the Musée du Louvre in Paris, which was inaugurated in 1793. Indeed, when reviewing the history of museum buildings, there are certain key moments when a new building signals an innovation or a dramatic change from past examples.

Looking back to the nineteenth century, a crucial moment in the history of museum architecture occurred with the realization of the Dulwich Picture Gallery, completed in 1814 by Sir John Soane, which so ingeniously allowed natural light to illuminate paintings from above. Karl Friedrich Schinkel's Altes Museum in Berlin (1823–30) also contributed to museum-building typology with its classical façade and central rotunda where visitors could congregate before entering the galleries. Without a doubt, Frank Lloyd Wright's controversial design for the Solomon R. Guggenheim Museum in New York (1946–59) can also be cited as the first time that architecture itself was as important as the works of art in contributing to the visitor's overall experience. Ludwig Mies van der Rohe took the Bauhaus concept of the neutral box to the extreme in the Neue Nationalgalerie in Berlin (1962–68) – it is the model for a universal building that can function as many types, not just as a museum. Among the more recent buildings that indicate a profound leap in thinking about museums is the Centre national d'art et de culture Georges Pompidou in Paris (1971–77). Designed by Renzo Piano and Richard Rogers, the innovative building signaled the beginning of visiting museums as a popular leisure activity, on a par with and in competition with other forms of recreation. The Pompidou was conceived as a cultural complex to be used at all hours of the day and night: as a gathering place, an event, and a vibrant part of the city that seemingly dissolves the boundaries between community and building. Finally, Frank Gehry's Museo Guggenheim Bilbao, which opened in 1997, has extended the time-honored definition of the museum to include its value as an icon for an entire city. In its expanded role, Gehry's museum in Bilbao has already become a memorable trademark for the Guggenheim, one as definitive as Wright's landmark in New York City. The Museo Guggenheim Bilbao functions as a marketing device, monument, symbol, and spectacle, as well as a repository for art.

The question of the lasting impact of the museum in Bilbao and other recent examples on museums to come can only be ascertained over time, with the appropriate historical distance and analysis. What is clear today, though, is that current museums must grapple with much more complex mission statements than museums of two hundred or even fifty years ago. The number of museums built in the last twenty years rivals the number built in the previous one hundred. This increase in building activity has also fueled more debates about the role of museums in society and, therefore, places increased demands on the architecture of museums.

The ways in which an architect embraces a museum – its collection, its role within the city, and its diverse functions – become crucial to the design of the museum. This was especially the case for Rafael Moneo when he designed the Audrey Jones Beck Building of the Museum of Fine Arts, Houston, because the proposed building presented multiple challenges. One concern was adding a new building to an existing museum campus – an institution identified not only by its acclaimed collection of world art, but also by the distinguished architectural entities that make up the building complex. The decision to hire Moneo was reached after a careful search that considered thirty prominent architects, including Tadao Ando, Norman Foster, and Frank Gehry. The selection of Moneo in 1992 was based on his voiced concerns and his understanding of the intended harmonious relationship between the building and the variety of historical artworks to be displayed. Equally important was Moneo's considerable experience and successful track record in building museums.

Moneo, born in Tudela, a village in the Navarre region of northern Spain, studied architecture at the Escuela Técnica Superior de Arquitectura de Madrid at a time when the six-year professional degree program was so demanding that many students never completed it or needed more than ten years to do so. He also spent two years as a fellow at the Academia di España in Rome, which undoubtedly enhanced his appreciation for history and the classical roots of architecture. In the 1960s he taught in Madrid and then accepted a tenured position from the Escuela Técnica Superior de Arquitectura de Barcelona. Since the 1970s, Moneo had also become known in architectural circles for his work as a theoretician, contributing to the avant-garde publication *Arquitecturas bis*, which originated in Barcelona. In 1976, he was invited to be a visiting fellow at the Institute for Architecture and Urban Studies in New York City. Yet he was relatively unknown outside these spheres. This limited recognition was a condition suffered by virtually all Spanish architects of that time. Moneo's name became more familiar to American audiences when he was appointed chair of the architecture department at Harvard University's Graduate School of Design in 1985. This appointment coincided with a period of intense activity at his atelier in Madrid. When Moneo was asked if the timing was right to accept even more obligations, he came to the conclusion that Harvard could not be refused. More than an inability to decline the offer of a prestigious Ivy League school, Moneo's acceptance reflects a deep commitment to teaching and investigation that has consistently developed alongside his love for building. In recognition of his tremendous range as an architect and educator, Moneo was awarded the 1996 Pritzker Architecture Prize.

When Moneo was awarded the museum commission in Houston, he had already completed four museums and was building a fifth. Moneo's museum architecture constitutes an interesting series of projects that represents some of the best examples of his career of more than thirty years. Taken together, Moneo's museums fit comfortably within his overall body of work. Examined individually, each museum reveals some of his fundamental concerns. These are issues that surface repeatedly in his buildings, regardless of their spatial type or specific functions.

1. Sir John Soane, Dulwich Picture Gallery, 1814. Gallery space. (By Permission of the Trustees of Dulwich Picture Gallery; photo: Martin Charles.)
2. Karl Friedrich Schinkel, Altes Museum, Berlin, 1823 to 1830. Main façade. (Photo: Reinhard Görner.)

In this day and age of signature architecture, when the individual stamp of the architect is often readily apparent in formal aspects or decorative elements, Moneo's architecture conveys a subtler, less boastful style. His apparent rejection of »type« speaks to the careful reader, encouraging multiple layers of interpretation and even prompting one to »read between the lines«. This assessment is not meant to suggest that Moneo approaches each work arbitrarily. Rather, the underlying concerns and interests are ever present, while their formal expression assumes a range of articulation.

The Museo Nacional de Arte Romano, Mérida

The Museo Nacional de Arte Romano in Mérida, Spain, was built from 1980 to 1986. To date, it remains one of Moneo's finest achievements. Though immediately inspiring to all who enter the main exhibition hall and encounter its dramatic arches, this building has subtle complexities that are revealed upon further analysis. The rather large museum, constructed of brick and evoking the spirit of Roman building, fits within the modest scale of the city through Moneo's careful handling of the different façades, and it engages in a dialogue with the still-powerful remnants of ancient Rome nearby. The entrance façade is simple and straightforward, as indicated by the sole word »museo« carved in the white marble architrave. The administrative and service wing is punctuated by windows with shutters, establishing a more direct relationship between the street and interior spaces. The exterior of the main hall is distinguished by a series of buttresses, indicating the rhythm of the arches inside but disclosing little more. The windows along the upper edge imply natural light.

Upon experiencing the powerful character of the interior spaces, one can fully appreciate Moneo's role as constructor. Although the building's structure is concrete faced with brick, in no way does it seem false. The dimensions, color, and positioning of the brick grant a sense of permanence and timelessness to the interior spaces. No special gallery finishes have been created; the works of art rest naturally against the brick surfaces in the bays. Elevated walkways lead the visitor to view the works on the upper level while offering the opportunity to experience the entire nave. The light that enters through the windows at the roof line adds to the drama of the main hall and intensifies the visitor's understanding of space and time.

Constructed on an archaeological site, the museum is built around the existing ruins, and from the lower level, one can view them in subdued light. Through this work, Moneo creates an eerie yet powerful juxtaposition of the ancient and the new.

The Fundació Pilar i Joan Miró, Palma de Mallorca

It is particularly telling that, in an article by Moneo on the design process for the Miró Foundation, he devotes more than half of the text to a description of the area, its physical characteristics, and the history of Joan Miró's construction of his house, designed by his brother-in-law, Enric Juncosa, in 1949 when Miró returned to Mallorca to live, and his studio, designed by Josep Lluis Sert in 1955. When Moneo arrived on the scene in 1987, he was understandably horrified by the aggressive way in which the neighboring buildings encroached on a site that once would have afforded unobstructed views of the Mediterranean Sea and the foothills of the interior of the island.

Moneo understood that the new museum building had to be protected, and thus he set about to create an inner world, one that would shut out the vulgarity of the surroundings. The building, completed in 1991,

consists of two main parts that are highly differentiated: the linear portion, which houses the study center, and the star-shaped gallery. The modest white wall, which is the back façade of the study center, leads the visitor toward the entrance and the stairs to the garden. This path also continues on to Miró's studio. From the building's entrance, one sees water, not in the distance but within the compound, on the roof of the gallery. Pushing up out of the pool are prismatic skylights.

The star-shaped gallery has little to do with the surrounding constructions; it is independent and fortress-like. When one enters the museum, a new environment is revealed. From the entrance, which opens at the highest level, the visitor can look down onto the irregularly shaped, flowing exhibition spaces that are illuminated by natural and artificial light. Daylight is mediated by concrete louvers, alabaster membranes, and overhead skylights. Moneo's architecture ensures that one is not distracted by the surroundings and can focus on the garden and Miró's sculpture through the open, low windows.

The Museo Thyssen-Bornemisza, Madrid

In a palace designed in the eighteenth century, with its present Neoclassical façades dating to the nineteenth century, Moneo undertook a complete reorganization of the building to house the Baron Thyssen-Bornemisza's esteemed art collection. The collection is on loan to Spain through an agreement between the baron and the Spanish Ministry of Culture. Prior to Moneo's project, the interior of the building had been compromised during its use as a bank. Moneo completed the building in 1992, and if one calls out the exceptional features of this work, the list would include the preparatory spaces, the organization of space and circulation patterns, the use of light, and the scale of the rooms as they relate to the artwork.

Moneo placed the new entrance within the small garden on the north side of the building. The visitor makes the transition from the bustling urban street to a semi-private area, and, upon entering the building, finds a large, rather empty space lit from above, where the second moment of readiness occurs. From this place, one can begin to understand the size, scale, and organization of the building before ascending to the top floor to commence viewing the collection.

The organization of the top-floor galleries creates a combination of intimacy and procession. A continuous corridor, so to speak, is open along the façade of the museum with partition walls placed perpendicular to it. The openness of the rooms, sized appropriately for viewing small groups of paintings, is particularly comfortable. Natural light enters through the windows, and their rhythm enhances the rhythm of the gallery spaces. Light also enters the inner galleries from above through a series of lanterns located in the central portion of the museum's roof.

One descends the staircase, or elevator, to the second floor. Again, this procession builds anticipation for the experience of viewing the next selection of artwork, which is of a different historical period. Finally, the auditorium and auxiliary services are located below ground level, thus segregating these more utilitarian aspects from the inspirational experience of viewing art.

The Davis Museum and Cultural Center, Wellesley College, Wellesley, Massachusetts

Moneo was selected from a long list of possible architects to receive Wellesley College's commission for the Davis Museum and Cultural Center. He embarked on the design in 1989 and completed the building in 1993. Although Moneo had close connections to the United States through the academic positions he had

3. Rafael Moneo, Museo Nacional de Arte Romano, Mérida, Spain 1980–86. Interior. (Photo: Lluis Casals.)
4. Rafael Moneo, Fundació Pilar i Joan Miró, Palma de Mallorca, Spain, 1987–91. General view. (Photo: Duccio Malagamba.)
5. Rafael Moneo, Fundació Pilar i Joan Miró. Interior. (Photo: Lluis Casals.)
6. Rafael Moneo, Museo Thyssen-Bornemisza, Madrid, Spain, 1989–92. Exterior. (Photo: Ana Muller.)
7. Rafael Moneo, Museo Thyssen-Bornemisza, Madrid, Spain. Interior. (Photo: José Latova, ASF Imagen.)

held, the Davis Museum marked his first commission to build in this country. About the complex at Wellesley College, he has stated that he »would like the Davis Museum to be understood as working with Paul Rudolph's Jewett Art Center and with the campus. This is not a lavish building. It does not present you with a sense of richness. And yet there is a richness in the ample scale of the galleries. Here at Davis, even though we are talking about rooms, the spaces are not enclosed. They escape toward the higher ceiling of the upper floor ... the cubic volume of the Davis Museum is like a coffer: the artworks of the collection are like the memories of those alumnae who lived here, therefore I wanted the museum to be like a treasury.«[1]

Moneo's first concern was the siting of the Davis Museum. Respectful of both the Rudolph structure and the intentions of the Frederick Law Olmsted landscape design for the campus, Moneo located the new construction to the west, creating a better view of Jewett and honoring its place within the college campus. This decision also allowed the existing stair to be connected to the new complex by creating a piazza in front of it, thus energizing and defining a space to be used in a meaningful way. In response to the small site, the new museum building is a cube that rises up five levels and is crowned with skylights.

Inside the building, the staircase is a fundamental element. It works functionally, splitting the cube into two parts and forming two different sizes of gallery space. The staircase also contributes to the viewing experience, creating a procession from one gallery to another, allowing appropriate time for the visitor to make a thoughtful transition from one artistic experience to the next, while still offering the freedom to choose which galleries to visit.

Although Moneo claims that the building is not lavish, the defined spaces, the choice of materials – a brick exterior, simple white interior walls, maple casework, and staircase paneling – and the effects of the overhead lighting make it a visually rich environment, indeed.

The Moderna Museet and the Arkitekturmuseet, Stockholm

An international competition of the early 1990s, open to all Swedish architects and to five international architects invited to participate, resulted in Moneo winning the commission to design the new buildings for the Moderna Museet and the Arkitekturmuseet on the island of Skeppsholmen. The site for the art museum, partially cleared by the demolition of a former structure, is an elongated stretch of land next to a building that was once an old ropery. The architecture museum is housed partially in a building that was previously reserved for exhibiting modern art as well as in a new adjacent building. The intent was to affect minimally the fragile and delicate existing architecture of the island. Moneo proposed an architecture that is »discontinuous and broken, as is the city of Stockholm, always respecting and incorporating a geography rich in accidents to which architects adapt, creating a picturesque and lively atmosphere.«[2] The result is an irregularly shaped building, held together on one side by a long spine, which provides the main circulation route for arriving at the entry-level galleries.

Because of the requirements for housing highly diverse holdings – contemporary Swedish painting and sculpture, avant-garde works from the 1950s to the 1970s, the architecture collection, and works featured in temporary exhibitions – the flexibility of the interior spaces became a crucial factor. Moneo's solution was to create clusters of rectangular and square galleries that change in their proportions as well as in their dimensions. The gallery ceilings on the main floor are pyramidal and contain skylights, again demonstrating the

architect's long-standing concern for using both natural and artificial light for viewing painting and sculpture. From an aerial perspective, the skylights bob up from the roof and indicate the variety of the museum's interior spaces. However, the skylights do more than illuminate the interior. The roof is a vital part of the landscape. In the extreme Nordic climate, known for its extended absence of daylight, the lanterns become veritable beacons in the dark, and the light emitted enhances the exterior and the overall presence of the building.

The Audrey Jones Beck Building of The Museum of Fine Arts, Houston, Texas

Moneo was hired in the fall of 1992 to begin designing the new Audrey Jones Beck Building, intended to house the museum's collections of the art of antiquity; masterworks of European art; Renaissance and Baroque works from the remarkable collection of the Sarah Campbell Blaffer Foundation; the acclaimed John A. and Audrey Jones Beck Collection of Impressionist and Post-Impressionist Art; prints, drawings, and photographs; and American paintings, sculpture, and decorative arts before 1945. The Beck Building is perceived as the culmination of the museum's recent expansion program, which has occurred over the last fifteen years and includes the Lillie and Hugh Roy Cullen Sculpture Garden, created by Isamu Noguchi in 1986, and the Glassell Junior School of Art and the central administrative building, designed by Carlos Jiménez in 1994.

Moneo was faced with a site across Main Street from the Caroline Wiess Law Building, designed by Ludwig Mies van der Rohe, and bordered by Binz, Fannin, and Ewing streets on the remaining sides. A master plan, defined by Denise Scott Brown of Philadelphia's Venturi Scott Brown and Associates in 1980, stipulated a main face on Binz, following the cues marked by the Mies building. At first glance, this approach may seem a logical path to follow: adding two new buildings whose façades become part of the sequence of façades along the street and are to be read as a series. The master plan acknowledged the difficulty of »developing a coherent, civil, and ceremonious public realm within the pattern of Museum-owned properties, existing open spaces, and arterial traffic.«[3] The suggested siting would have maintained a constant façade height along Bissonnet to Binz. There was also a design that established a continuous arcade to link the new buildings on Binz and provide large outdoor spaces.

Moneo, however, questioned these premises and reevaluated the site. He opted to pursue a more realistic approach for the task at hand. Given that the existing museum buildings are seen as separate parts of an overall scheme – the entire campus stretches across more than seven city blocks – it would be difficult to create links among old and new or even among two or three new structures by positioning low, connected façades on Binz, as suggested in the master plan proposal. The current buildings are, instead, fine examples of various styles, all commissioned by the museum, which together form a unique complex of architectural significance. They are pieces in a collection. The original building is a Beaux-Arts structure designed in 1924 by William Ward Watkin. In 1953 Mies was asked to design an extension which resulted in two new buildings – the Cullinan Hall, completed in 1958, and the Brown Pavilion, completed in 1974. Although these two buildings are connected, each has a powerful façade, which leads to understanding the buildings as separate personalities. It seems as if Moneo enjoyed what might be described as the »risky coexistence« of the two architectural styles and wanted to participate in the dialogue. Without a doubt, the architect's enormous respect and admiration for the work of Mies al-

8. Rafael Moneo, Davis Museum and Cultural Center, Wellesley College, Wellesley, Massachusetts, 1989–93. General view. (Photo: Scott Frances/Esto, 1993.)
9. Rafael Moneo, Davis Museum and Cultural Center. Interior. (Photo: Steve Rosenthal.)
10. Rafael Moneo, Moderna Museet and Arkitekturmuseet, Stockholm, Sweden, 1991–98. General view. (Photo: Duccio Malagamba.)
11. Rafael Moneo, Moderna Museet and Arkitekturmuseet, Stockholm. Rooftop lanterns. (Photo: Belén Moneo.)

so led him to create the main entrance and façade on Main Street, directly opposite the original buildings. By reinforcing the Main Street side, more attention is granted to the museum and less to the church across the street on Binz – another factor in Moneo's decision.

Fulfilling the extensive program requirements and guided by a desire to create an urban structure, Moneo has defined a dense building that occupies almost the entire site and extends three stories above ground and one below. Perhaps it is also the hand of Moneo the European, the admirer of Renaissance palaces, that has created a vertical building for this site. The new building, a rectangle that intensively uses the available land by following the exact outline of the plot, seems almost confined by its bordering streets. The four street façades, clad in the same Indiana limestone employed in other buildings of the Museum of Fine Arts, Houston, are rather austere and dignified. The roof, however, is well articulated – a rich landscape formed by the many skylights protruding upward – and could be described as a model for a city itself. Of note is how the configuration of the lanterns echoes the downtown Houston skyline seen in the distance. The building itself is a statement, just as all of the previous buildings of the museum campus are. The Beck Building is one addition to this collection, much more than a mere backdrop or unifying element.

Ever mindful of the importance of the car in America and especially in a city like Houston, where driving great distances daily is a way of life, Moneo dealt with Houston's car culture in a straightforward manner. A drop-off area for cars is handled gracefully and does not disrupt the architecture of the main façade. (The City of Houston stipulated that the museum provide parking facilities, and a separate structure for 327 cars has been built on the adjacent block across Fannin Street.) Large, monolithic letters, designed by Massimo Vignelli in concert with Moneo, spell out »Museum of Fine Arts, Houston«, and form part of the outer wall of the Main Street façade. In a direct way these letters and the deep red-colored granite are a sign, indicating the principal entrance, but are also much more than mere decoration, as they form part of the structure itself. The museum also commissioned sculptor Joseph Havel to create two monumental bronze reliefs. The work titled *Curtain* flanks the Main Street entrance and welcomes visitors at the principal point of entry. *Curtain* masterfully evokes the ceremonial nature of entering a grand space.

The other three façades of the Beck Building are treated independently, in response to the condition of the streets and the interior activities. Binz Street has a secondary entrance, indicated by a canopy proportioned for pedestrian traffic. Water, which flows from street level down to the restaurant below, is also used here. Fannin Street is articulated by service access at street level and windows on the mezzanine level. The »box« is also slightly modified to allow for a row of clerestory windows that permit light into the American art galleries on the ground floor. The Ewing Street façade, facing the neighboring hotel, is even more subdued.

To deal with the complexities of installing the permanent collection and exhibiting more works from the collection of the Sarah Campbell Blaffer Foundation, as well as providing the support facilities needed for a museum of this size, an adjacent 231,000-square-foot parking and service facility, called the MFAH Visitors Center, was included in the building program established by the museum. The facility, designed by Kendall Heaton, under the supervision of Moneo, contains the central heating, cooling, and humidifying plant; loading docks; non-art storage; workshops; special events and retail offices; and a large ticketing and orientation lobby. The visitors facility, accessible via an underground connection to the Beck Building, evolved as the museum's programmatic needs expanded. As

a result, the four-story Beck Building, measuring a total of 192,447 square feet, can use its privileged position exclusively for art, public amenities, curatorial offices, and study space for the works on paper collection. More than 85,000 square feet of the new building is dedicated to gallery space.

Inside the building, the museum is conceived as a varied and complex collection of rooms. This concept is in striking contrast to the apparent regularity of the exterior. On the second floor, there are 28 galleries for European art, along with a small education gallery and a conservation studio. Each area of the permanent collection is displayed in its own group of rooms, dimensioned specifically to present the works of art to their best advantage. The floor plan resembles a labyrinth and is conducive to the visitor pursuing multiple paths, permitting and even encouraging different routes. The emphasis is on the individual's choice, recognizing that viewing and contemplating art is a highly personal endeavor.

The skylight lanterns on the roof allow natural light to illuminate the second-floor galleries. According to Moneo, the lanterns are »machines to capture light«. Though not a new invention (Soane designed the Dulwich Gallery using natural light from above, which enters in vertical and diagonal rays and is diffused by the arched ceiling, and Moneo previously used rooftop lanterns for the Thyssen-Bornemisza and Stockholm museums), the skylight has certainly been perfected at Houston. The skylights consist of a glass lantern that penetrates the roof to catch the light. The lanterns are covered on the outside by steel louvers that moderate the light and also protect the glass in the event of high winds. Between the lantern and the gallery's interior ceiling is a throat, or collar, portion that mixes the light and filters out potentially damaging UV rays. The daylight that arrives in the galleries can be supplemented with artificial light and is remarkably consistent regardless of the changing seasons or the sun's location throughout the day.

The materials used for the galleries are quiet and enduring and help to create spaces that are domestic in character. Oak floors contrast with the subtle colors on the walls. Brushed bronze doorways mark the passage from one gallery to another. Once in a while, Moneo suggests that the visitor connects with the outside, offering a glance through a window toward the Mies building or up toward the light entering from above to illuminate the American Sculpture Court.

The ground floor of the building is an activity area, providing a distinct contrast to the quieter atmosphere of the second-floor galleries. As one would expect, centered around the entrance are the museum shop, ticket counter, information desk, and coatroom. The main circulation means are also here: escalators lead down to the restaurant and a smaller changing exhibition gallery. A little farther inside are the elevators and escalators that lead to the second floor. Although one enters the building at an area with a normal ceiling height, one takes only a few steps before encountering a soaring atrium, lit by a skylight from eighty feet above. The visitor's sight is immediately drawn upward.

The atrium of the building is a preparatory space, not in the classical sense of the museum where one is quiet and anticipating the artistic experience, but a

12. William Ward Watkin, Caroline Wiess Law Building, The Museum of Fine Arts, Houston, 1924. (Photo: Hester + Hardaway.)
13. Isamu Noguchi, Lillie and Hugh Roy Cullen Sculpture Garden, The Museum of Fine Arts, Houston, 1986. (Photo: Hester + Hardaway.)
14. Carlos Jimenez, Glassell Junior School of Art and Central Administration Building, The Museum of Fine Arts, Houston, 1994. (Photo: Hester + Hardaway.)
15. Mies van der Rohe, Caroline Wiess Law Building, The Museum of Fine Arts, Houston, 1958–74. (Photo: Aker/Zvonkovic Photography LLP.)

continuation of city life. In function, the atrium is more like the foyer of a theater, creating an opportunity for gathering and socializing as visitors orient themselves. It is also an area where the building is revealed. The cube, interpreted from the outside as solid, now becomes more understandable and inviting. The entire left side of the atrium is dedicated to an Indiana limestone wall incised with the names of the museum's major donors. The light walls contrast with the Dakota mahogany granite floor. The design of the ground-floor galleries, with their high ceilings and generous spaces, is flexible enough to accommodate the display of a wide variety of artworks. The ground floor also features an 8500-square-foot gallery designated for traveling exhibitions.

On the lower level, traveling to the Caroline Wiess Law Building and the MFAH Visitors Center is resolved via tunnels. »Tunnel« is the appropriate term for the long passageway to the visitors facility; however, the below-ground connection to the Law Building has the dimensions of a gallery. Artist James Turrell was commissioned to create one of his »Shallow Space Constructions« for this tunnel space, which he entitled »The Light Inside«. Here, the walls are illuminated vessels, and one especially appreciates the museum's selection of an artist who, like Moneo, is deeply concerned with space and light.

Moneo has taken the measured approach in his design of the Audrey Jones Beck Building. The new museum is conscious of its urban context and seeks to be even »more urban« than some of its neighbors. Moneo is respectful of the work of previous architects in his positioning of the building, his use of exterior and interior materials, and his articulation of the façades.

The museum does not seek to be a monument: the only hint of monumentality is witnessed in the atrium. Moneo has commented that because so much of Houston is monumental in scale, the size loses its value and then is seen as normal. Perhaps the architect did not want to compete on this front, but it is more likely that he thought a monumental scale would not serve the collections effectively. He has created a dignified building and has made a noble contribution to the architectural campus of the Museum of Fine Arts, Houston. When experiencing the Audrey Jones Beck Building, and recognizing how the architecture responds to the works of art, one has the feeling that the pleasures of contemplating artistic masterpieces are foremost in Moneo's mind. The careful use of natural light, radiating from the numerous lanterns above, inspires and reminds us that we, like the centuries of art displayed, are part of a larger whole.

Notes

[1] Rafael Moneo, »Davis Museum, Wellesley College«, A+U, 294 (March 1995), p. 69.
[2] Rafael Moneo and Johan Mårtelius, Modern Museum and Swedish Museum of Architecture in Stockholm, Stockholm: Arkitektur Förlag and Rasyer Förlag, 1998, p. 18.
[3] Venturi Scott Brown and Associates, Museum of Fine Arts, Houston, Master Plan, 1990, p. 25.

Selected bibliography

Writings by Rafael Moneo on other architects and theoretical considerations

»Aldo Rossi: The idea of architecture and the Modena cemetery«, *Oppositions*, no. 5 (summer 1976), pp. 1–30. – This article was written in Spanish in 1973 soon after Rossi won the competition to design the cemetery. It is published in English for the first time in *Oppositions*.

Bovisa. John Hejduk, Cambridge: Harvard University Graduate School of Design, 1987. – The large-format exhibition catalogue of the drawings of John Hejduk opens with a text by Rafael Moneo. He offers a personal interpretation of Hejduk's work and its ciphered messages. Moneo touches on themes present in the drawings and points out some of the problems facing the discipline that Hejduk confronts through his drawings.

»4 Citas/4 Notas« (»Four Quotes/Four Notes«), *Arquitecturas bis*, nos. 38/39 (July/October 1981), pp. 44 to 48. – This article, first published in 1981, was reprinted in 1996 in a book titled *Aprendiendo de todas sus casas*, published by the Valles Division of the Catalonia School of Architecture. The four quotes that Moneo analyzes refer to different architects' and critics' views of the career and work of Sir John Soane. Moneo's text is published in Spanish only.

»Introduction«, in: Michael K. Hays and Carol Burns, eds., *Thinking the Present: Recent American Architecture*, New York: Princeton Architectural Press, 1990.– The publication, the result of a conference held at Harvard University's Graduate School of Design, examines American architecture of the previous twelve years. Throughout his text Moneo challenges architects, critics, and historians to fill in the gaps and look critically and theoretically at the architecture of the present.

»On typology«, *Oppositions*, no. 13 (summer 1978), pp. 22–44. – This article is an in-depth theoretical discussion of »type« and its value for understanding the nature of the architectural object. Moneo traces different interpretations of typology throughout history and the use or rejection of the concept, critically pondering the question: »Does it make sense to speak of type today?«

»Postscript«, in: Peter Arnell and Ted Bickford, eds., *Aldo Rossi, Buildings and Projects*, New York: Rizzoli, 1985. – Moneo wrote this analysis of the architecture of Aldo Rossi as the final text in the 1985 monograph on the work of Rossi. Moneo's eloquent text is a lasting tribute from one architect to another.

»The contradictions of architecture as history«, *Architectural Design (Profile*, 42) 52 (1982), nos. 7/8, p. 54. – Moneo argues that any attempt to understand architecture as a linear and continuous history is doomed because of architecture's very nature and the confluence of realities affecting it.

»Third Manfredo Tafuri Lecture«, *Casabella*, no. 653 (February 1998), pp. 42–51. – The text of a memorial lecture given in Venice by Moneo in which he traces and analyzes architectural criticism and theory from Sigfried Giedion through Robin Evans and Christine Smith.

»Unexpected coincidences«, in: *Wexner Center for the Visual Arts. Ohio State University: A Building Designed by Eisenman/Trott Architects*, with an introduction by Edward H. Jennings, New York: Rizzoli, 1989. – Moneo analyzes the Wexner Center, designed by architect Peter Eisenman. He compares it to Eisenman's previous work and highlights the shift toward a concern for site and context.

Books on Spanish architecture that include references to Rafael Moneo

Güell, Xavier, *Spanish Contemporary Architecture: The Eighties*, Barcelona: Editorial Gustavo Gili, 1990. – The book provides an overall view of new buildings in Spain in the 1980s and presents twenty-eight examples from around the country, with texts in English and Spanish. Moneo's office building for an insurance company in Seville is illustrated, and Joseph Rykwert singles out Moneo in his introduction, calling him a master who is well known and internationally respected.

Saliga, Pauline, and Martha Thorne, eds., *Building in a New Spain*, Madrid: Ministry of Public Works and Transports, 1992. – A general overview of Spanish architecture from 1985 to 1992 includes analytical texts and twelve representative buildings. Moneo's Seville airport is featured in this catalogue, which accompanied an international exhibition of the same title.

Solà-Morales, Ignacio, ed., *Contemporary Spanish Architecture: An Eclectic Panorama*, New York: Rizzoli, 1986. – Moneo's National Museum of Roman Art at Mérida, Spain, is featured on the cover of this exhibition catalogue, which examines three decades in the evolution of Spanish architecture. Kenneth Frampton's introduction situates Moneo within the broad context of Spanish and international architecture

Books and monographs on the work of Rafael Moneo

Architecture, 83, no.1 (January 1994), pp. 45–85. – The issue opens with text by Kenneth Frampton and proceeds with a profile of Moneo's work, highlighting the Atocha Railway Station, the Miró Foundation, the Thyssen-Bornemisza Museum, and the Davis Museum and Cultural Center.

Granell, Enrique, ed., *Bankinter 1972–1977*, Almeria: Colegio de Arquitectos de Almeria, 1994. – This small-format book details the development and completion of the Bankinter building, considered one of Moneo's most important works. The book also reprints five critical texts published in various Spanish journals of the time. Although the texts are published in Spanish only, all readers will enjoy the creative design of the book.

José Rafael Moneo, Fundación Pilar i Joan Miró. Almeria: Colegio de Arquitectos de Almeria, 1996. – This small-format book is part of the *Documentos* series of publications on individual works or architects. The text, published originally in *D'A* (a now defunct journal), is reproduced in English and Spanish and reveals the architect's initial concerns about and the processes used in the design of this building. Numerous illustrations provide a better understanding of the architecture of the Miró Foundation.

Nigst, Peter, *Rafael Moneo: Bauen für die Stadt* (Building for the City). Stuttgart: Verlag Gerd Hatje, 1993. –

An exhibition catalogue presenting works that range from Moneo's 1973 housing design in San Sebastian to the Kursaal Cultural Center project of 1990. The black-and-white illustrations in the book (with text in German) provide a good overview of twelve of the architect's major projects.

»Rafael Moneo«, *A+U*, no. 227 (August 1989), pp. 27 to 134. – This monograph is the most comprehensive publication to date that is devoted to the architect's body of work through 1989. Of special interest are the article by Francesco Dal Co on the museum in Mérida and Moneo's own text, »The Solitude of buildings«.

»Rafael Moneo, 1986–1992«, *AV Monographs*, no. 36 (July/August 1992), pp. 1–112. – The journal, originating in Madrid, features Moneo's work from 1986 to 1992, including five completed buildings and annotated with commentaries by the architect. The monograph contains excellent critical texts by Alan Colquhoun, Luis Fernandez Galiano, Colin Rowe, and Daniele Vitale, all of which are available in an English or a Spanish edition of the journal.

»Rafael Moneo, 1987–1994«, *El Croquis*, no. 64 (1994). – A lavish monograph published by the Spanish architectural journal on some of Moneo's major works, accompanied by texts in English and Spanish by William Curtis and Josep Quetglas, respectively, and an interview with the architect.

Rafael Moneo and Johan Mörtelius. Modern Museum and Swedish Museum of Architecture in Stockholm. Stockholm: Arkitektur Fårlag and Rasyer Fårlag, 1998. – A handsome book published for the opening of Stockholm's new museums designed by Moneo. The texts in English and Swedish include a critical analysis of the new project by Mörtelius and brief descriptions by Moneo of this building and his other museum projects. The book concludes with a thorough analysis, supplemented by plans and color photos of the museum complex.

Journal articles on Rafael Moneo

Bertolucci, Carla, »Murcian civitas«, *The Architectural Review*, no. 1229 (July 1999), pp. 67–72. – The addition to the city hall of Murcia, Spain, is thoughtfully described and illustrated with plans and color photographs. The author places special emphasis on how the new building fits within the existing context.

Buchanan, Peter, »Moneo Romana, Mérida Museum, Mérida, Spain«, *The Architectural Review*, no. 1065 (November 1985), pp. 38–47. – A thoughtful analysis of Moneo's lasting monument in Mérida, the article includes a discussion of the character and function of the space, construction techniques, and building materials.

Büttner, Ulrich, »Sensibel eingefügt« (Sensibly placed), *md*, July 1998, pp. 24–29. – Plans, photos, and brief texts in English, German, and French provide an introduction to the Swedish museums.

Capezzuto, Rita, »Modern art and architecture museums complex, Stockholm«, *Domus*, no. 806 (July/August 1998), pp. 18–27. – Stockholm's museum complex is thoroughly analyzed and richly illustrated in color.

Ericsson, Edith, »Nordic Lantern«, *The Architectural Review*, no. 1221 (November 1998), pp. 36–41. – A straightforward text along with plans and photos introduces Moneo's new Stockholm building, placing special emphasis on the landscape created by the new museum and its careful insertion into the existing site.

Fernández-Galiano, Luis, »Profesor Moneo«, *AV Monographs*, nos. 63/64 (January–April 1997), pp. 194 to 199. – The author argues that Moneo is a professor, above all: not only in the strict sense of the word, but also in a broad sense, due to the lessons that his architecture teaches. The author then looks at ten buildings by Moneo and comments on their »lessons« through texts in English and Spanish.

Frampton, Kenneth, »Light is the theme: Museum of Modern Art and Architecture, Stockholm«, *AV Monographs*, no. 71 (May/June 1998), pp. 12–27. – Frampton, whose text is published in English and Spanish, methodically describes Moneo's museum, pointing out what he believes are some of its disconcerting effects.

Germany, Lisa, »In Houston, a museum that speaks for itself«, *The New York Times*, 31 October 1999.

»The idea of lasting: a conversation with Rafael Moneo«, *Perspecta*, no. 24 (1988), pp. 146–157. – In an interview with the editors of *Perspecta*, Moneo presents some of his ideas on the concepts of abstraction, materiality, and ephemerality and discusses the National Museum of Roman Art in Mérida.

Morteo, Enrico, »Rafael Moneo: l'interno del Museo d'Arte Romana a Mérida«, *Domus*, no. 690 (January 1988), pp. 52–61. – In a beautifully illustrated article with texts in English and Italian the author focuses on the interior furnishings, details, and exhibition supports designed by Moneo and explores how they work within the powerful space of the museum in Mérida.

»Rafael Moneo, Davis Museum, Wellesley College«, *A+U*, no. 294 (March 1995), pp. 68–99. – Drawing on excerpts from an interview, Moneo discusses his design criteria for Wellesley College's museum. The article is generously illustrated with sketches, plans, and photographs.

»Rafael Moneo, Museums of Modern Art and Architecture, Stockholm, Sweden 1991–1997«, *A+U*, 337 (October 1998), pp. 16–35. – In an issue of the journal devoted to Madrid architects soundly rooted in a modern tradition, the new Swedish museum by Moneo is presented in plans, diagrams, and photographs showing many new views of the complex. Plans and model photographs of Our Lady of the Angels Cathedral in Los Angeles are also included in this issue.

»Rafael Moneo: New Municipal Building«, *Casabella*, no. 666 (April 1999) pp. 20–27. – Rafael Moneo's design for a municipal building set in a square defined by a baroque cathedral is examined. In addition to the plans and photographs of the building, two brief, critical texts by Jean-Marie Martin and Francisco Jarauta discuss the composition of this work.

Sherr, Leslie, »Site as signature: Rafael Moneo«, *Graphis*, no. 52 (November/December 1996), pp. 152 to 155. – A brief profile of Moneo the architect, teacher, and critic.

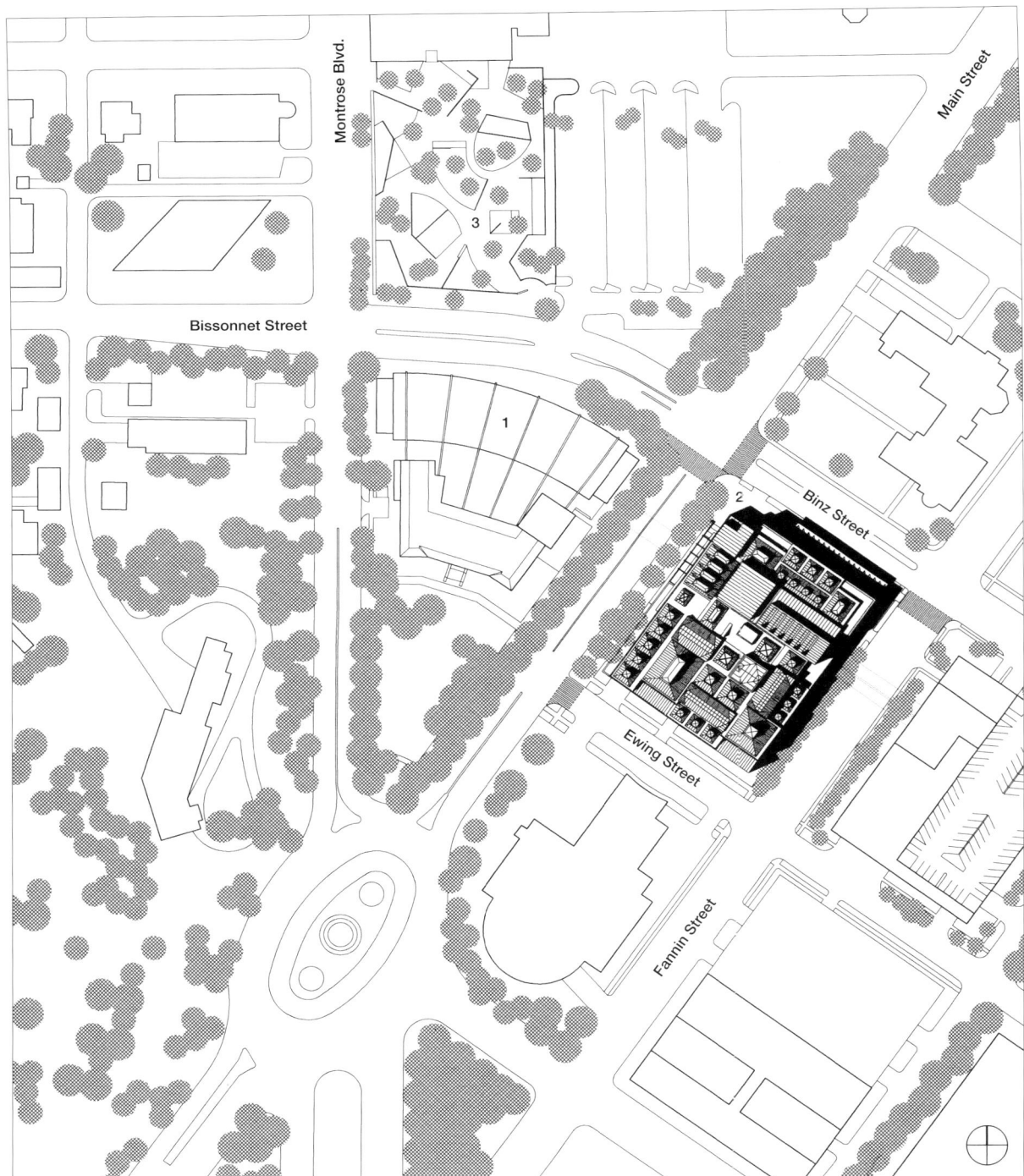

1. Area map. Key: 1 Caroline Wiess Law Building, 2 Audrey Jones Beck Building, 3 Lillie and Hugh Roy Cullen Sculpture Garden.
2, 3. Floor plans (ground floor, gallery floor).

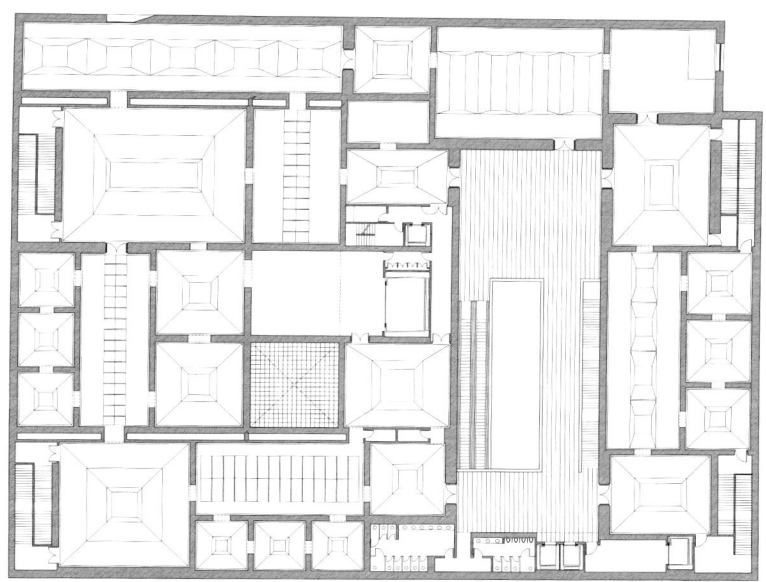

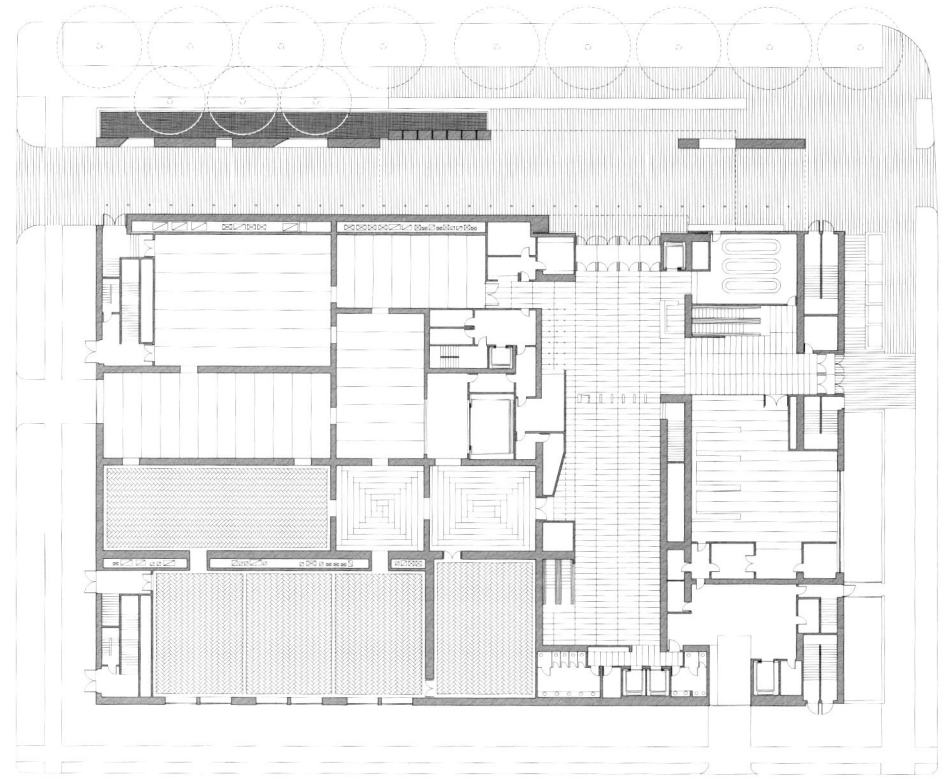

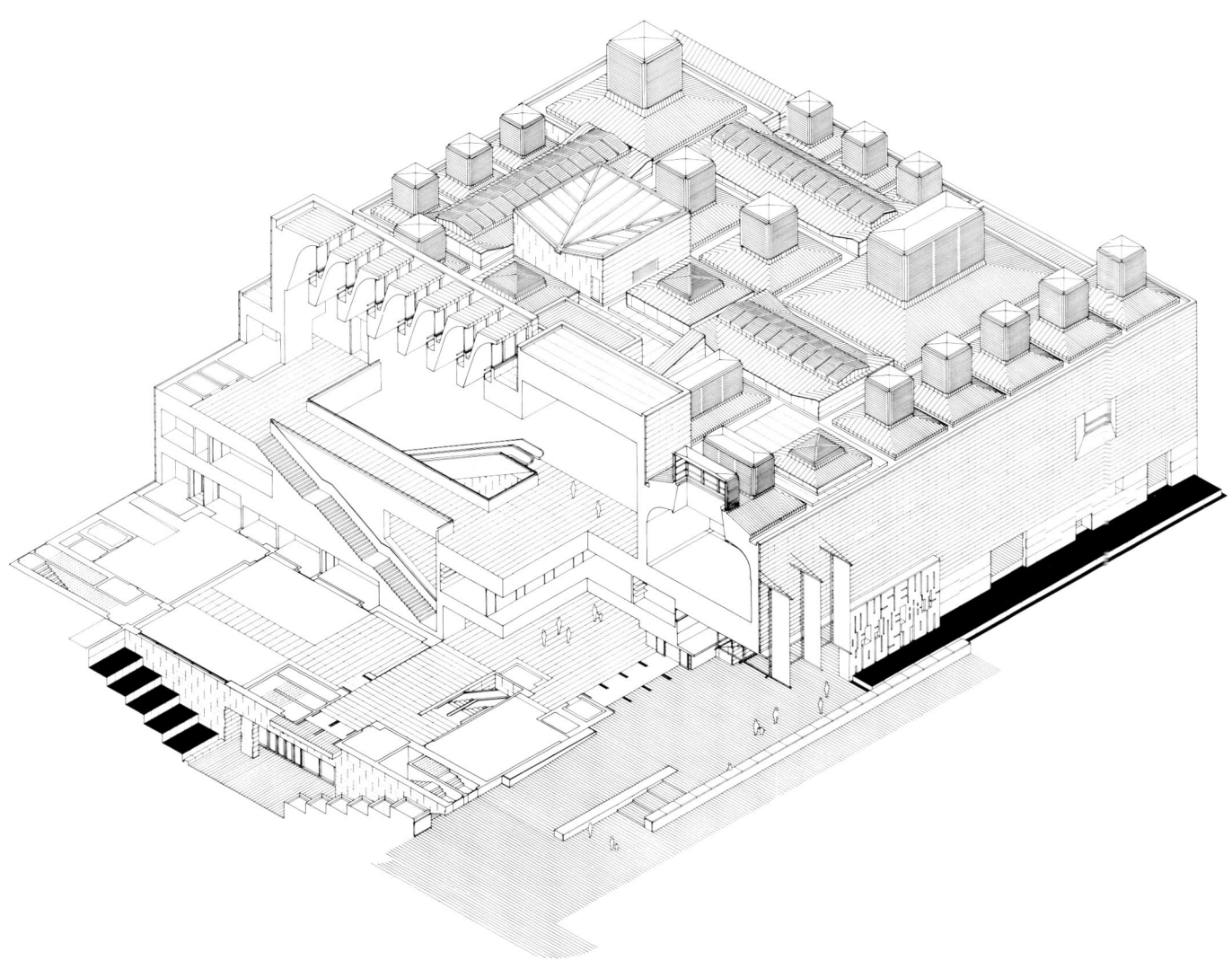

4. Axonometric section.
5. Axonometric view.

p. 126/127
6, 7. Sections.

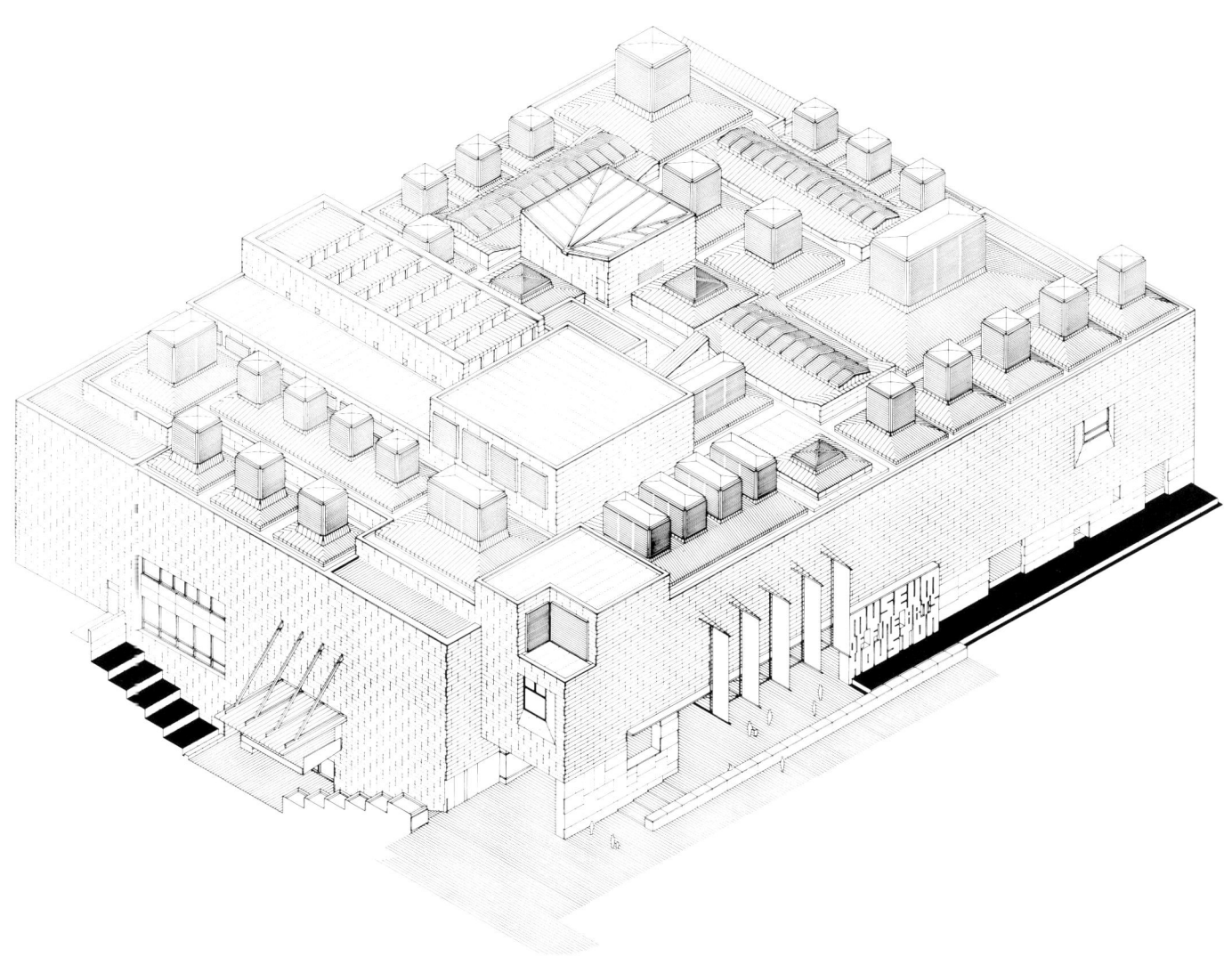

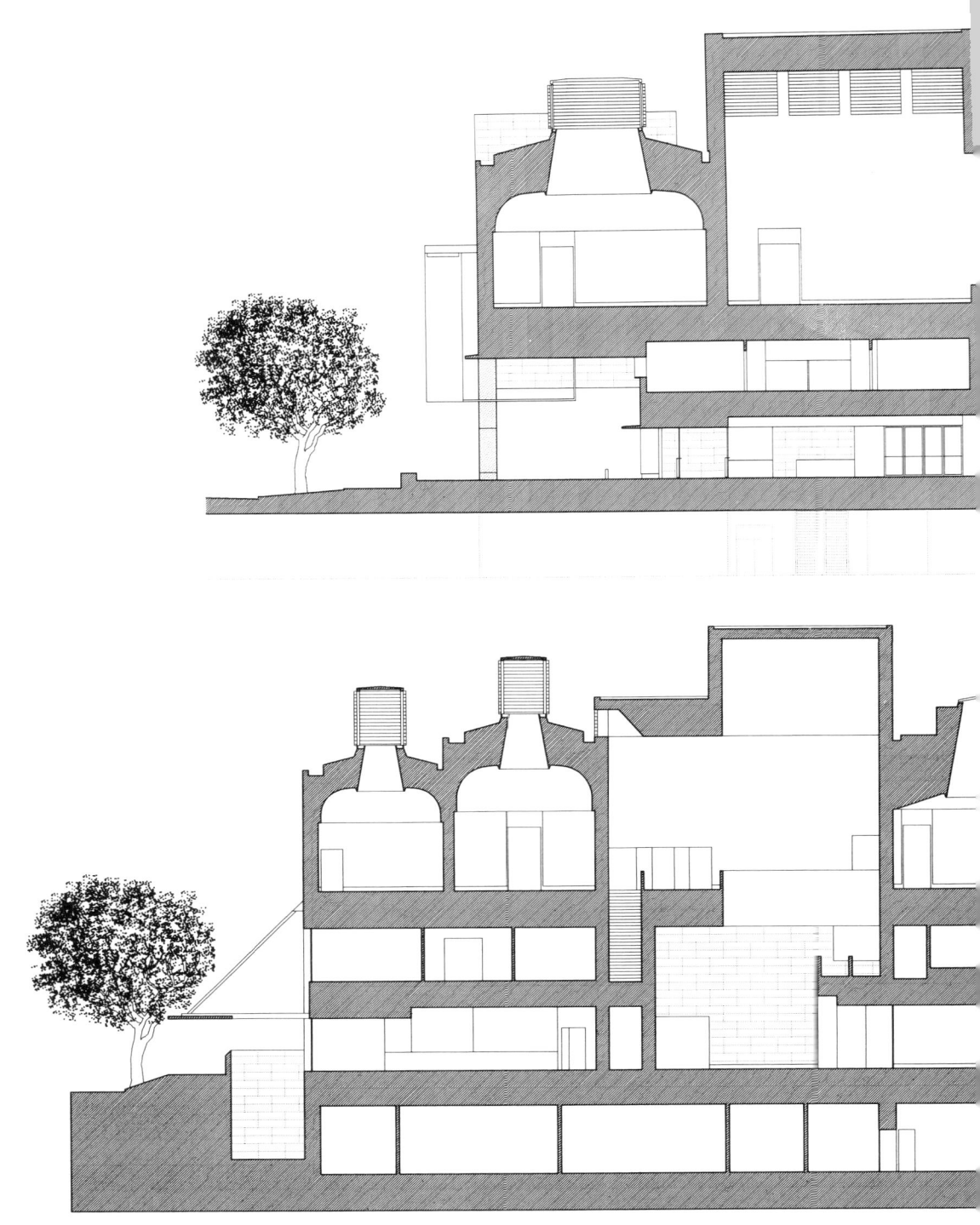

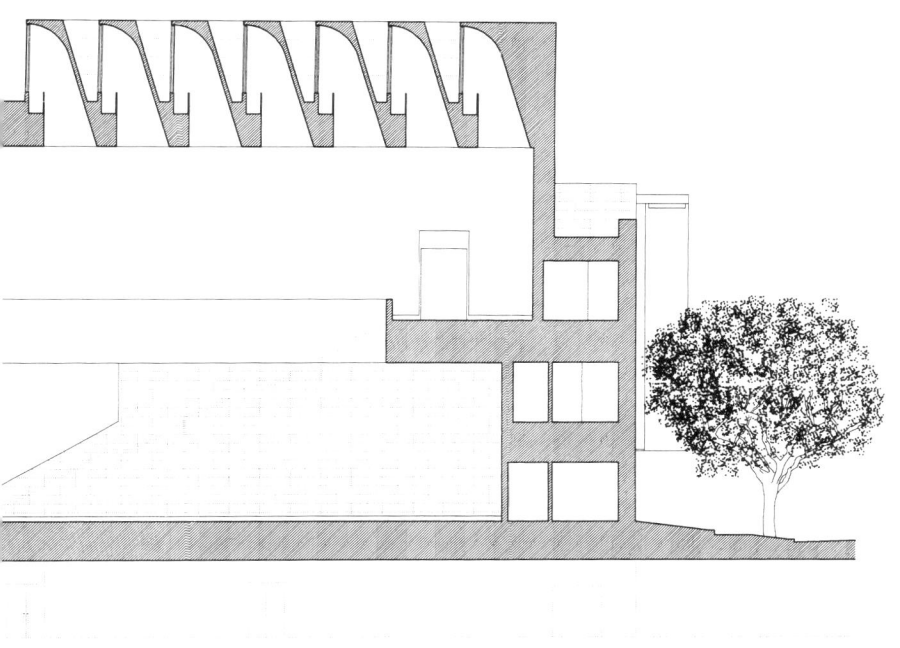

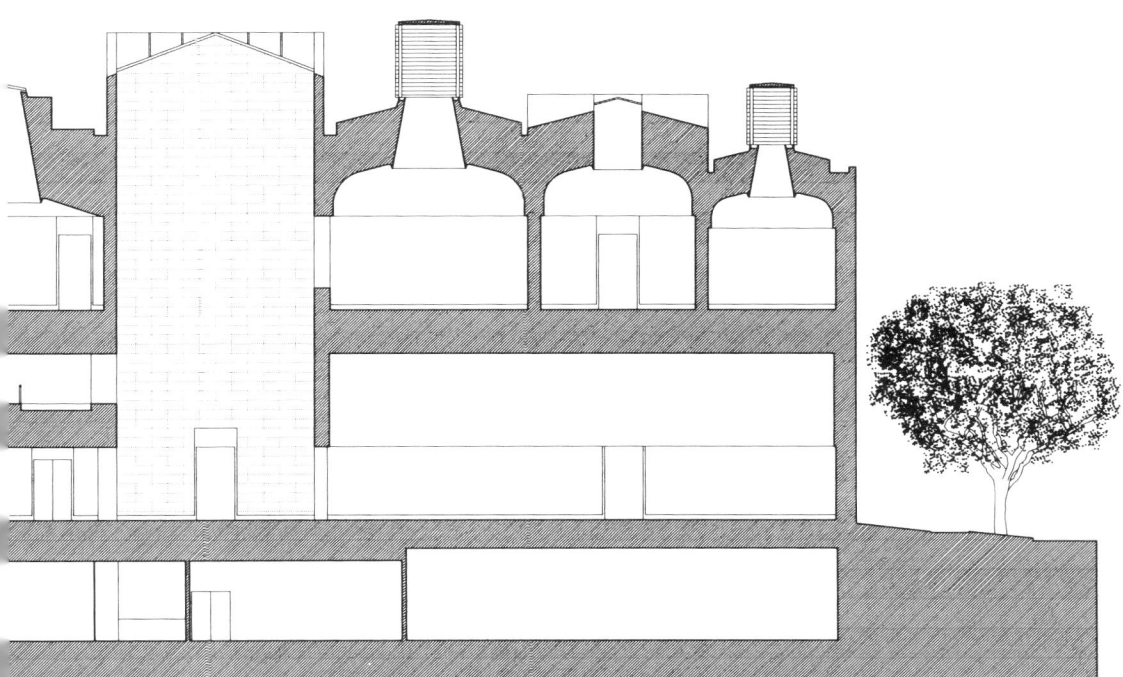

p. 128/129
1. Aerial view of the Beck Building with the Law Building to the right.

2. View of the Beck Building from Fannin Street.
3. View of the MFAH Visitors Center and Parking Garage from the intersection of Fannin and Binz Streets.
4. View of the MFAH Visitors Center and Parking Garage and the Beck Building from Binz Street.

5, 6. View of the building from Main Street with architectural banners enhancing the main entrance.
7. View of the building from Binz Street.

p. 134/135
8. View of the building from the intersection of Main Street with Binz Street and Bissonnet Street.

9, 10. Close-ups of rooftop lanterns.
11. Detail view of the façade facing Ewing Street with rooftop lanterns.

p. 138, 139
12, 13. Detail views of the façade facing Main Street with main entrance.

p. 140, 141
14. Main entrance at Main Street.
15. Side entrance at Binz Street.

16, 17. Covered passageway along Main Street with main entrance.

18. View of the atrium from the Main Street entrance.
19. The atrium looking toward the lobby and the Main Street entrance.

20, 21. Detail views of the atrium.

22, 23. The upper atrium.

p. 150/151
24. Galleries of American Art. Room on the Ewing street side featuring *A Wooded Landscape in Three Panels*, c. 1905, by Louis Comfort Tiffany, Tiffany Studios, New York.

25. Gallery for works on paper and photography on the Fannin Street side.
26. Galleries of American Art. Gallery on the Fannin Street side.

27. Galleries of European Art. Gallery adjacent to the atrium on the southwest side.
28. Galleries of European Art. Gallery on the Ewing Street side.

29. Galleries of European Art. Gallery on the Main Street side with installation in process.

30, 31. Galleries of European Art. Galleries on the Main Street side with installation in process.

p. 160, 161
32. Galleries of European Art. Gallery above the entrance on the Main Street side with installation in process.
33. Galleries of European Art. Gallery on the corner of Main and Binz Streets with installation in process.

34. Galleries of European Art. Gallery adjacent to the atrium on the northeast side with installation in process.
35. Galleries of European Art. Gallery west of the atrium with installation in process.

p. 164/165
36. Rooftop lanterns framing a view of Houston's downtown skyline.

The Audrey Jones Beck Building
Museum of Fine Arts
Houston

Client
The Museum of Fine Arts, Houston
Director: Peter C. Marzio
Owner's representative: Gwendolyn H. Goffe

Design architect
José Rafael Moneo, Arquitecto, Madrid
Staff: Eduardo Miralles

Production architect
Kendall/Heaton Associates, Inc., Houston
Principal-in-charge: Laurence C. Burns, Jr.
Staff: Steve Bell, John Goodman

Sarah Campbell Blaffer Foundation consulting architect
Eubanks Group Architects, Houston
Principal-in-charge: Edwin Eubanks

Landscape architect
Clark Condon Associates, Houston
Principal-in-charge: Sheila Condon

Project consultant
Hines, Houston
Executive vice president: Louis Sklar
Vice president: Fred Jenkins

Graphics
Vignelli Associates, New York
Principal-in-charge: Massimo Vignelli
Staff: Peter Vetter, Yoshiki Waterhouse

Mechanical engineers
Altieri Sebor Wieber, Norwalk
Principal-in-charge: Andrew Sebor
Project engineer: Vladimir Goldin
Plumbing: Jay Kohler, Robert Cancian
Fire protection: David Lussier
Electrical engineer: Joseph Pawell
Field inspector: Joseph Pappolla

Structural engineers
CBM Engineers, Inc., Houston
Principal-in-charge: Joseph Colaco
Senior structural consultant: Wally Ford

Lighting design
Fisher Marantz Renfro Stone, New York
Principals-in-charge: Paul Marantz, Richard Renfro
Staff: Alicia Kapheim, Hank Forrest

Builder
W. S. Bellows Construction Corporation, Houston
President: Tom Bellows
Vice president: Don Jones
Project manager: Bob Higgins
Superintendent: Robert Knox
Project engineer: Brent Miller

Gottfried Knapp
Raumfiguren für die Kunst – Heinz Tesars Museumsbau für die Sammlung Essl in Klosterneuburg

Wer sich ohne nähere Kenntnis des Ortes auf der unscheinbaren Zubringerstraße dem hoch geschlossenen, langgezogenen Architekturgebilde nähert oder es per Zufall vom vorbeifahrenden Zug aus entdeckt, wird dessen Zweck wohl schwerlich erraten. Mit den bekannten Grundtypen heutigen Bauens, mit Wohn-, Industrie-, Verwaltungs- oder Sakralbauten hat diese Rätselarchitektur kaum etwas gemein. Sie muß eher ungewöhnlichen Aufgaben dienen. Und tatsächlich umschließt das Gebäude etwas, was man hier, im chaotisch verbauten Gewerbegebiet zwischen Bahndamm und Donauauen, am wenigsten erwartet: ein Museum zeitgenössischer Kunst, ein Kulturforum, wie es in dieser Form in Europa bisher nicht existiert hat. Das auffällige Gebäude beherbergt die wohl umfassendste Privatsammlung neuerer Kunst in Österreich. Es wird in jeder Hinsicht privat, also ohne öffentliche Zuschüsse betrieben; dennoch ist es mit allem ausgestattet, was zu einem repräsentativen Museum gehört: mit Depots, Restaurierungswerkstätten, einer eigenen Museumsmannschaft und auch dem nötigen Betriebskapital.

Agnes und Karlheinz Essl haben als junge Leute in Amerika das generös-mäzenatische Wirken der Oberschicht kennengelernt und erste Erfahrungen mit den bildenden Künsten, mit dem amerikanischen Galeriensystem, mit Kunstfreunden und Künstlern gemacht. Nach ihrer Rückkehr aus den USA und nach der Heirat trat Karlheinz Essl in das Unternehmen seines Schwiegervaters Schömer in Klosterneuburg ein und begann jene Kette von Heimwerkermärkten mit dem Namen »bauMax« aufzubauen, die heute in Österreich und Osteuropa führend ist.

Das Sammeln von Kunst wurde zur zweiten Profession der Eheleute Essl. Innerhalb von 30 Jahren haben sie eine Sammlung aufgebaut, die zumindest auf dem Gebiet der neueren österreichischen Kunst ohne Konkurrenz ist. Und von Anfang an war es ihnen eine Selbstverständlichkeit, die wachsenden Schätze in Katalogen zu publizieren und der Öffentlichkeit in Ausstellungen zugänglich zu machen. So sind bedeutende Teile der Sammlung im Auftrag des österreichischen Ministeriums für Auswärtige Angelegenheiten als kulturelle Botschafter um die ganze Welt gereist.

Im Jahr 1990 machten die Essls dann dem österreichischen Staat das Angebot, ihre Sammlung in das geplante Museumsquartier auf dem Gelände der ehemaligen Hofstallungen in Wien zu überführen. Ihre Idee war, hierfür den von den Museumsarchitekten vorgeschlagenen, aber in der Öffentlichkeit umstrittenen »Bücherturm« als Galeriegebäude zu nutzen und so ein wesentliches Element des Gesamtplans für das kulturelle Großunternehmen des Landes zu retten. Doch die von der Presse aufgehetzten Gegner des kühnen Unternehmens hatten sich in der Öffentlichkeit bereits darauf festgelegt, den Turm nicht zu bauen. Es war den Politikern offensichtlich nicht bewußt, daß sie mit ihrer Ablehnung eine Sammlung von Weltrang, die den Bilderbestand der teuer erworbenen Sammlung Leopold auf dem gleichen Niveau bis in die Gegenwart verlängert hätte, aus Wien vertrieben. Für die Essls war die Ablehnung durch den Staat der Anlaß, an ein eigenes Ausstellungshaus und an ein zentrales Bilderdepot in der eigenen Stadt zu denken und so der mäzenatischen Arbeit in Klosterneuburg eine neue Dimension zu geben.

Schon seit 1987, seit der Eröffnung ihres neuen Verwaltungszentrums, des Schömer-Hauses in Klosterneuburg, zeigten die Essls in der eigens dafür konzipierten zentralen Halle Teile der Sammlung; sie organisierten ambitionierte Einzelpräsentationen für Maler ihrer Wahl wie Arnulf Rainer, luden Aktionskünstler wie Hermann Nitsch zu höchst spektakulären Aktionen ein und öffneten das Haus für die Neue Musik: Unter der Leitung ihres Sohnes, des Komponisten Karlheinz Essl junior, wurden höchst anspruchsvolle internationale Avantgardekonzerte veranstaltet, ja sogar Kompositionsaufträge vergeben.

Den einzigartigen Rahmen für all diese vielfältigen künstlerischen Aktivitäten – das Schömer-Haus – hatte Heinz Tesar entworfen. Und da der Bau viel gelobt wurde, lag es nahe, daß sich die Mäzene auch bei ihren anderen Stiftungswerken wieder mit dem eigenwilligen Wiener Künstler-Architekten zusammentaten, der beim Schömer-Haus so viel raumästhetisches Gefühl, so viel Bewußtsein für die Belange der Künste gezeigt hatte. So kam es zu der gloriosen Dreiheit von Kult- und Kulturbauten in jener Stadt bei Wien, die bis dahin nur ihres grandiosen Augustiner-Chorherrenstiftes und der darin bewahrten mittelalterlichen Kunstschätze wegen im Bewußtsein der kunstinteressierten Weltöffentlichkeit existiert hatte.

Für die gläubigen Protestanten Agnes und Karlheinz Essl – auch das haben sie in den USA studieren können – war der erworbene Besitz immer auch eine Verpflichtung gegenüber der Öffentlichkeit. In einem Gespräch hat Karlheinz Essl einmal gesagt: »Besitz bedeutet Verantwortung. Das kommt aus meiner protestantischen Überzeugung heraus. Ein Teil von dem, was wir erwirtschaften konnten, soll wieder einer breiteren Öffentlichkeit zugute kommen.«

Wie das geht, haben die Essls zunächst mit dem Kulturprogramm im Schömer-Haus vorgeführt. In den neunziger Jahren haben sie dann weitere kräftige Zeichen gesetzt: Sie haben den Bau einer neuen evangelischen Kirche in Klosterneuburg ermöglicht und ihren eigenen Kunstbesitz in eine Stiftung überführt, die den ständig wachsenden Bestand bewahren und in einem eigenen Ausstellungshaus der Welt vermitteln sollte. Und da sie die Architektur für diese beiden neuen Projekte wieder Heinz Tesar anvertrauten, rundete sich die Arbeit des Architekten in Klosterneuburg zu einem höchst anspruchsvollen Gesamtkomplex, den man nur als Glücksfall für die Architektur empfinden kann.

Bevor wir uns etwas eingehender mit dem Haus der Sammlung Essl beschäftigen, wollen wir zunächst kurz die beiden mit diesem spannungsvoll kommunizierenden und kontrastierenden Vorläuferbauten in Klosterneuburg betrachten.

Das Schömer-Haus, in dem die Hauptverwaltung des »bauMax« sitzt, gibt sich nach außen als Verwaltungsbau zu erkennen, nimmt also die temporäre Zusatzfunktion als Kulturforum ganz ins Innere zurück. Der viergeschossige, symmetrisch gegliederte Kubus auf rechteckigem Grundriß ist in den einzelnen Stockwerken mit minimalen Mitteln – mit raffinierten Kurvierungen – geschickt differenziert. So tut sich über dem Haupteingang eine dreigeschossige Nische mit kurvierter Rückwand auf. Auf der Rückseite springt das Kasino im Erdgeschoß wie ein Mittelrisalit mit einer kon-

Gottfried Knapp
Spatial figures for art – Heinz Tesar's museum building for the Essl Collection in Klosterneuburg

Anyone approaching this long, tall, closed architectural structure on the unassuming access road or discovering it by chance from a passing train will have difficulty in working out what it is for. This mysterious architecture has scarcely anything in common with modern building's familiar basic types for housing, offices or churches. It must be for some unusual purpose. And indeed the building does contain something that is most unexpected here, in the chaotically ill-built commercial area between the railway line and the meadows by the Danube: it is a museum of contemporary art, a cultural forum that has so far not existed in this form in Europe. This striking building contains what is probably the most comprehensive collection of recent art in Austria. It is private in every respect, that is to say it is run without any public subsidy; and yet it has everything that one associates with a prestigious museum: storage space, restoration workshops, its own museum team and also the necessary working capital.

Agnes and Karlheinz Essl became familiar with the generosity with which upper-class Americans give patronage to the arts while spending time there as young people, and gained their first experience of fine art, the American gallery system, art-lovers and artists. After coming home from the United States and getting married, Karheinz Essl joined his father-in-law Schomer's business in Klosterneuburg and start to build up the chain of do-it-yourself stores called »bauMax«, which is now a market leader in Austria and Eastern Europe.

Collecting art became a second profession for the Essls. They have built up a collection over thirty years that is unequalled, at least in the field of recent Austrian art. And from the outset they took it for granted that they should publish their accumulated treasures in catalogues and make them accessible to the public in exhibitions. Thus significant parts of the collection have travelled the world as cultural ambassadors on behalf of the Austrian Ministry of Foreign Affairs.

In 1990 the Essls suggested to the Austrian state that they would be prepared to place their collection in the planned museum quarter on the site of the former court stables in Vienna. Their idea was to use the »Book Tower«, which had been proposed by the architects but had proved controversial with the public, as a gallery and thus rescue a fundamental element of the whole plan for the country's major cultural enterprise. But the opponents of this bold enterprise, who had been stirred up by the press, had already brought about a public decision that the tower should not be built. The politicians were obviously not aware that by this act of rejection they had driven a world-class collection out of Vienna. It would have complemented the Leopold Collection, which had been acquired at considerable expense, by providing contemporary art on the same level. For the Essls, rejection by the state made them think of an exhibition building of their own and a central repository for pictures in their home town, thus giving a new dimension to patronage of the arts in Klosterneuburg.

Ever since 1987, when their new headquarters, the Schömer-Haus in Klosterneuburg opened, the Essls had been showing part of the collection in the central hall, which was specially conceived for this purpose; they organized ambitious one-man shows for painters of their choice like Arnulf Rainer, invited action artists like Hermann Nitsch to create spectacular actions and opened up the building for new music: high-calibre international avant-garde concerts were put on under the direction of their son, the composer Karlheinz Essl junior, and some new music was even commissioned.

Heinz Tesar had designed the Schömer-Haus, which provided a unique frame for all these various cultural activities. And as the building had been much praised, it made sense for the patrons to team up with this unconventional Viennese artist-architect again, as he had shown so much sensitivity to space and aesthetics and so much awareness of the needs of art in the Schömer-Haus. And so that town near Vienna, which had hitherto been in the consciousness of the world public only for its wonderful Augustinian Chorherrenstift, and the medieval art treasures housed in it, now has a glorious trinity of ecclesiastical and secular buildings as well.

Agnes and Karlheinz Essl, who are practising Protestants, always saw the possessions they had acquired as giving them a commitment to the public – something else they were able to study in the USA. Karlheinz Essl once said in an interview: »Possessions mean responsibility. This comes from my Protestant convictions. Part of everything we have been able to obtain by careful management should benefit a wider public again.«

The Essls showed how this worked first of all with the cultural programme in the Schömer-Haus. They then set another powerful example in the nineties: they made it possible to build a new Protestant church in Klosterneuburg and placed their own art collection in a trust that was to look after the steadily growing body of work and display it to the world in a custom-built exhibition building. And as they once more put Heinz Tesar in charge of the architecture for these two new projects, the architect's work in Klosterneuburg became a highly prestigious complete project that can only be seen as a happy chance for architecture.

Before we look at the building for the Essl Collection in more detail, we would first like to look at the two earlier buildings in Klosterneuburg, which communicate and contrast with this excitingly.

The Schömer-Haus, which contains the headquarters of »bauMax«, looks like an office building from the outside, in other words it hides its temporary additional function as a cultural forum well away inside itself. The four-storey, symmetrically articulated cube on a square ground plan is skilfully broken down into individual floors using a minimum of resources – sophisticated curves. Thus there is a three-storey niche with a curved rear wall above the main entrance. On the rear side, the canteen leaps forward on the ground floor like a central projection with a concave curve in its façade, in the two storeys above this the outer wall curves outwards in a convex counter-movement, and on the fourth floor the four corners of the building are omitted so that four roof terraces with curved walls open up.

The outside walls follow various segment arcs, sometimes convex and sometimes concave, and there is a response to this in the interior from a huge, transverse-oval central hall rising through all four storeys, with galleries running round it, showing parts of the art collection at all times. This oval arena of the arts with

1. Heinz Tesar, Schömer-Haus, Klosterneuburg.
(Photo: Margeritha Spiluttini.)
2. Heinz Tesar, evangelische Kirche in Klosterneuburg.
(Photo: Mischa Erben.)
3. Heinz Tesar, Sammlung Essl, Klosterneuburg.
(Photo: Christian Richters.)

1. Heinz Tesar, Schömer-Haus, Klosterneuburg.
(Photo: Margeritha Spiluttini.)
2. Heinz Tesar, Protestant church in Klosterneuburg.
(Photo: Mischa Erben.)
3. Heinz Tesar, Sammlung Essl, Klosterneuburg.
(Photo: Christian Richters.)

kav gekurvten Front nach vorn, in den beiden Geschossen darüber wölbt sich die Außenwand in einer Gegenbewegung konvex nach außen, und im vierten Stock sind die vier Ecken des Gebäudes so ausgespart, daß sich dort vier Dachterrassen mit gekurvten Wänden auftun.

Den diversen Segmentbögen, denen die Außenwände mal konvex, mal konkav folgen, antwortet im Inneren eine durch alle Geschosse reichende riesige querovale Mittelhalle mit umlaufenden Galerien, an deren Wänden ständig Teile der Kunstsammlung ausgestellt sind. Diese ovale Arena der Künste wirkt mit ihren vier Rundumgalerien wie der moderne Nachbau eines Renaissance-Theaters – und wie in dieser Urform eines Zuschauerraums funktioniert auch die Akustik in der Halle so selbstverständlich, daß Konzerte jeder Größenordnung denkbar sind.

Überspannt wird das Oval, in dem schon ein kleines Stück Avantgarde-Geschichte geschrieben wurde, von einer flachen Decke, über der eine große runde Laterne zum Tageslicht emporragt und ein Kranz von kleinen runden Lichtkuppeln zusätzlich Oberlicht nach unten transportiert. Beherrschendes plastisches Element im Raum ist das in der Mittelachse mächtig in den Raum vorspringende zweiläufig-symmetrische Treppengehäuse, das mit seinen »Treillagen« – dem Lineament seiner senkrecht verlaufenden Metallstangen – und mit der oben aufsitzenden plastischen Figur den skulpturalen Anspruch des Architekten kräftig unterstreicht und daran erinnert, daß Tesar ja selber einmal bildnerisch tätig war, bevor er als Architekt bekannt wurde.

Im Schömer-Haus kommen sich also eine ausgeprägte Rationalität und eine fast obsessive Lust am eigensinnig geformten Detail, an bestimmten, immer wiederkehrenden Formen, höchst kreativ ins Gehege. Eine Folge von Fluren, die im Grundriß zusammen ein Rechteck bilden, verbindet im Inneren alle Arbeitsräume miteinander. In den Restflächen zwischen den

its four galleries running the full way round it seems like a modern copy of a Renaissance theatre, and as in this prototype of an auditorium the acoustics of the hall can be taken absolutely for granted, so that concerts of any size can function perfectly.

The oval, in which a little bit of avant-garde history has already been written, is spanned by a flat ceiling above which a large round lantern towers up to the daylight, and a garland of small round light-domes admit additional daylight from above. The dominant three-dimensional element in the space is the housing for the double-flighted, symmetrical staircase, which thrusts powerfully into the space on the central axis. Its »trelliswork« – the lines of its vertical metal rods – and the three-dimensional figure placed at the top powerfully underline the architect's sculptural aspirations and remind us that Tesar did indeed work in this field before he became known as an architect.

And so in the Schömer-Haus a marked sense of rationality and an almost obsessive delight in unconventionally formed detail, in certain shapes that constantly recur, are brought very creatively into play. A sequence of corridors, which together form a rectangle in the ground plan, links all the working rooms in the interior with each other. The lifts and toilets are accommodated in the spaces left between the surrounding corridors and the large, inscribed oval space. Thus the building is perfectly symmetrical in ground plan and elevation.

umlaufenden Fluren und dem einbeschriebenen großen Raumoval sind die Lifte und die Toiletten untergebracht. Im Grund- und Aufriß bietet sich das Haus also perfekt symmetrisch dar. Doch eine Fülle von weichen, gerundeten Formen, von Kreisen, Kreissegmenten und ihren Längungen ins Ovale, schneidet in die strenge Rechteckordnung ein, wölbt sich aus ihr heraus oder ist, wie in dem fischbauchförmigen Vordach über dem Windfang des Haupteingangs, den Geraden vorgelagert. Auch das Ineinander von Kreis und Oval, wie es an der Decke der zentralen Halle zelebriert wird, oder die gekurvten Zipfel, in die das Vordach an der Chefecke oder die Muster im Steinboden der Halle auslaufen, gehören zum persönlichen Formenvokabular Tesars, das in all seinen Bauten in individuellen Variationen zum Einsatz kommt.

Die evangelische Kirche in Klosterneuburg ist sogar ganz aus Rundformen entwickelt. Ein Oval umgibt den Gemeinderaum; aus ihm treten die Wände an der Schmal- und an der Breitseite je einmal in sanfter Weitung ein Stück weit heraus, so als würden sie zu einer Spirale ansetzen. Sie öffnen die Außenwand so, daß durch den Schlitz an der Schmalseite Licht in den gerundeten Altarraum fällt. Die andere, die breitere Weitung öffnet sich zum Kirchenvorplatz hin; sie dient als Eingang und als Vorraum für die Besucher.

In das Oval des Innenraums ist über dem Eingang eine kreisförmige Orgelempore als skulpturales Element eingefügt. Eine flache Längstonne wölbt sich als Decke über dem eiförmigen Raum; sie ist von 25 runden Lichtkuppeln durchbrochen. Ein originales Muster von Rechtecköffnungen in der gekurvten Südwand und rundum unter dem Gewölbeansatz bringt zusätzlich Licht herein. Der magisch geschlossene Kultraum bekommt also durch das Neben- und Ineinander verschiedener Rundformen und durch das hochindividuelle System der unterschiedlichen Lichtöffnungen seinen eigenwilligen Charakter.

Auch der dritte Bau, den Tesar im Auftrag der Familie Essl in Klosterneuburg errichtet hat, ist ein Solitär, auch er baut sich als geschlossene, plastisch differenzierte Einheit auf dem Grundstück. Das Haus für die Kunstsammlung Essl liegt ungefähr auf halber Strecke zwischen den kulturellen Fixpunkten des Ortes, dem Schömer-Haus und dem kuppelgekrönten barocken Prachtbau des Chorherrenstifts. Es bildet im Grundriß ein rechtwinkliges Dreieck, das mit seiner Hypotenuse parallel zur Bahntrasse verläuft und mit dem spitzen Winkel in Richtung Stift weist.

Hinter der kürzesten Seite, der nach Süden gerichteten, liegt der Eingangstrakt. Er enthält hinter der mit Fensterbändern gegliederten Fassade alle nicht unmittelbar für die Aufbewahrung und Präsentation der Kunstwerke bestimmten Funktionen: im Erdgeschoß die Eingangshalle für die Besucher mit Kasse und Garderobe sowie die Werkstätten und die Haustechnik; im ersten Zwischengeschoß Büros und eine Einliegerwohnung; im ersten Obergeschoß, dem Hauptausstellungsgeschoß, die durch zwei Stockwerke hinaufreichende Bibliothek; im zweiten Zwischengeschoß das ebenfalls zwei Stockwerke hohe Tonstudio für Karlheinz Essl junior; im zweiten Obergeschoß, dem Geschoß des Großen Saals, die Verwaltungsräume der Stiftung Essl mit einem turmartigen Aufbau an der westlichen Ecke schließlich ein Studio für Agnes Essl.

Der Aufzugsturm für diese fünf Geschosse ist als eigener Baukörper so vor die Fassade gestellt, daß schmale Lichtschlitze – wir werden ihnen noch öfter begegnen – zwischen Lift und Außenwand emporlaufen. Über eine leicht ansteigende Rampe betreten die Besucher das Erdgeschoß, das wegen des möglichen Donauhochwassers um einen Meter angehoben wurde. Aus der schlichten Kassen- und Garderobenhalle führt der Weg über die höchst reizvoll vor die senkrechten Lichtschlitze der Außenwand modellierte dreiläufige Treppe in das eigentliche Galeriegeschoß hinauf. Dort verlassen sie den Eingangstrakt und begeben sich in einen der beiden langgestreckten, nach Norden aufeinander zulaufenden Museumstrakte, die den begrünten Hof auf recht gegensätzliche Weise flankieren.

Was der Museumsbau in Klosterneuburg unter der hochgehobenen Plattform der Galerieräume birgt, kann alle staatlichen oder kommunalen Museen neidisch machen. In dem hohen, im Grundriß dreieckigen fensterlosen Sockel sind Depoträume von geradezu verschwenderischen Ausmaßen und vorbildlicher Funktionalität untergebracht. Kunsttransporter können auf der Ostseite so tief in das Depot hineinfahren, daß sie bei geschlossenen Toren über die Laderampen stufenlos entladen werden können. Im Depot hat Tesar eine zentrale Transportstraße mit seitlichen Aufbewahrungsräumen angelegt. Jede dieser Hallen enthält rechts und links eine dichte Folge querliegender beweglicher Bilderwände, die in den breiten Mittelflur herausgezogen werden können. Das Depot ist streng auf dem rechten Winkel aufgebaut, was bei dem dreieckigen Grundriß des Außenbaus zwangsläufig zu Konflikten führt. Tesar gleicht den kalkulierten Widerspruch dadurch aus, daß er im Depotgeschoß die Hypotenuse, die schräg verlaufende westliche Wand dreimal einknickt, also der inneren Rechteckordnung anpaßt, was außen als reizvolle formale Bereicherung empfunden wird und der zur Bahn gerichteten Fassade einen maschinenhaften Rhythmus, ja ein spürbares Tempo verleiht. Im Museumsgeschoß darüber läßt Tesar die Außenmauer ohne Unterbrechung durchlaufen, sie folgt also dort exakt der Hypotenuse des rechtwinkligen Grundrißdreiecks. Doch da die hier hintereinander geschalteten Galerieräume wie die Depoträume darunter an der Rechteckordnung der Katheten orientiert sind, gibt es in den sechs einander folgenden Galerieräumen zwangsläufig jeweils eine Wand – die Außenwand –, die schräg verläuft. Die Räume sind daher im Grundriß trapezförmig und schieben sich mit ihren rechteckigen Kopfseiten unterschiedlich weit in den Hof vor, so daß sich dort eine eigentümliche Staffelung ergibt.

Diesen Teil des Museumstraktes hat Tesar als Galerie, als eine Abfolge klassischer Oberlichträume ausgebaut. Und da die Lichtöffnungen in den Decken genau der Raumform anpaßt, haben auch die aufgesetzten Laternen trapezförmige Grundrisse.

Bei der Belichtung variiert Tesar das von Leo von Klenze für die Alte Pinakothek in München entwickelte und bis heute kaum jemals übertroffene Oberlichtsystem auf recht suggestive Weise. Die hohen mächtigen Laternen, die wie Gewächshäuser auf dem Galerietrakt stehen, sind nach oben geschlossen. Sie nehmen durch ihre vier gläsernen Wände das Tageslicht auf. Jalousien auf der Außenseite und bewegliche Stoffvorhänge auf der Innenseite sorgen dafür, daß Sonnenstrahlen nicht direkt ins Innere dringen können. Das Licht wird also schon in der Laterne diffundiert und fällt als gleichmäßige, aber intensive Helligkeit in die Räume hinunter. Und da die Wände an ihren oberen Enden

But an abundance of soft, rounded forms, of circles, segments of circles and their elongations into ovals cut into the strict, square order, come curving out of it or are placed in front of straight lines, as in the fish-bellied canopy above the porch of the main entrance. Also linked circles and ovals, as celebrated in the roof of the central hall, or the curved tips into which the canopy on the management corner or the patterns on the stone floor of the hall run out are part of Tesar's personal formal vocabulary, which is used in individual variations in all his buildings.

The Protestant church in Klosterneuburg is in fact developed entirely from rounded forms. An oval surrounds the area for the congregation; from it the walls on the narrow and broad sides are each shifted outwards in a gentle widening movement that looks as though they are starting to form a spiral. They open up the outer wall in such a way that the slit on the narrow side admits light in the rounded chancel. The other, wider extension opens on to the square in front of the church; it serves as an entrance and an anteroom for visitors.

A circular organ-gallery is fitted into the oval of the interior as a sculptural element above the entrance. A shallow longitudinal barrel curves across the ovoid space to form the ceiling; it is pierced by 25 round light-domes. An unusual pattern of rectangular openings in the curved south wall and all the way around under the level at which the ceiling starts to rise provides additional light. The magically closed devotional room thus derives its unconventional character from the juxtaposition and interlinking of various curved forms and also from the highly individual system of different openings to provide light.

The third building that Tesar has built for the Essl family in Klosterneuburg is also a solitaire, and it too rises from its site as a closed, three-dimensionally differentiated unit. The building for the Essl Collection is roughly half-way between the town's fixed cultural points, the Schömer-Haus and the magnificent domed, Baroque building of the Chorherrenstift. Its ground plan is a right-angled triangle, with its hypotenuse parallel with the railway line and the acute angle pointing in the direction of the Chorherrenstift.

The entrance section is behind the shortest façade, which faces south. Behind the façade, which is articulated with continuous windows, it contains all the functions not directly concerned with storing and presenting the works of art: on the ground floor is the entrance hall for visitors with box office and cloakroom, and also the workshop and technical equipment; on the first mezzanine floor are offices and a flat; on the first floor, the main exhibition floor, is the library, which rises through two storeys; on the second mezzanine floor is the sound studio for Karlheinz Essl junior, which is also two storeys high; and finally on the second floor, which accommodates the Great Hall, the offices for the Essl Foundation and finally a studio for Agnes Essl in the tower-like structure on the west corner.

The lift tower for these floors is a building in its own right placed in front of the façade in such a way that narrow lighting slits – and we are going to come across these with increasing frequency – run up between the lift and the outside wall. Visitors come into the ground floor, which is raised by a metre because of possible flooding from the Danube, via a shallow ramp. The way out of the modest hall with box office and cloakroom leads via the three flights of stairs, charmingly placed in front of the vertical light slits in the outside wall, into the actual exhibition floor. There they leave the entrance section and move into one of the two long museum sections, running towards each other in a northerly direction, and flanking the planted courtyard in quite contrasting ways.

Any national or municipal museum would be envious of what the museum in Klosterneuburg has hidden away under the raised platform of the galleries. The tall, windowless base storey, triangular in ground plan, contains storerooms on an almost extravagant scale, that function in a model fashion. Art transporters can drive so deep into the store on the east side that they can be unloaded continuously via the loading ramps, with the main doors closed. Tesar has provided a central transport route with storerooms at the side in the store. To the right and left of each of these halls is a dense sequence of transverse walls for pictures, which can be pulled out into the broad central hall. The store is built rigorously on the right angle, which inevitably leads to conflicts, given the triangular ground plan of the outside building. Tesar balances out this calculated contradiction by introducing three bends into the hypotenuse, the west wall, which runs diagonally, on the store floor, in other words adapts it to the interior square order, which is seen as an attractive formal enrichment on the outside and gives the façade facing the railway a mechanical rhythm, indeed a detectable tempo. On the museum floor above this Tesar causes the external wall to run through without interruption; thus here it follows the hypotenuse of the right-angled triangle of the ground plan precisely. But as the gallery rooms, which are placed one behind the other here, like the storerooms below them, are oriented to the right-angled order of the legs of the triangle, in each of the six galleries following one after another there is inevitably one wall – the outside wall – that runs diagonally. The rooms are thus trapezoid in ground plan, and their right-angled ends thrust into the courtyard to different extents, which produces a strangely staggered effect.

Tesar has developed this part of the museum section as a gallery, as a sequence of classical rooms with top-lighting. And as he adapted the light openings in the ceiling precisely to the shape of the room, the lanterns on top are also trapezoid in plan.

In terms of lighting, Tesar varies the top-light system developed by Leo von Klenze for the Alte Pinakothek in Munich, which has scarcely been bettered down to the present day, in a very powerful fashion. The tall, massive lanterns, standing on the top of the gallery section like greenhouses, are closed at the top. They take in daylight through their four glazed walls. Blinds on the outside and fabric curtains that can be drawn on the inside make sure that sunlight cannot penetrate directly into the interior. Thus the light is already diffused in the lantern, and falls evenly, but with intense brightness, into the rooms. And as the walls make a smooth transition to extensive volutes at the top, in other words curve almost imperceptibly towards the lantern shafts, thus produces a wonderfully soft transition between wall and ceiling, without any shadows or dark places.

Tesar had concerned himself intensively with artistic themes and the way in which they can be presented in museums before starting to work as an architect, and thus found a highly subtle solution for the eternal prob-

kantenlos in weit ausholende Vouten übergehen, also sich den Laternenschächten fast unmerklich entgegenwölben, ergibt sich ein wunderbar weicher Übergang zwischen Wand und Decke, der keine Verschattungen, keine dunklen Stellen kennt.

Tesar, der sich, bevor er als Architekt zu arbeiten begann, intensiv mit bildnerischen Themen und mit ihrer Präsentation im musealen Zusammenhang beschäftigt hatte, fand somit in Klosterneuburg eine höchst subtile Lösung für das ewige Problem der Belichtung von Ausstellungsräumen. In vielen der architektonisch einprägsamen Museumsneubauten der letzten dreißig Jahre sind geradezu groteske Experimente gemacht worden, um das Tageslicht einzufangen und zu lenken. Tesar schlägt sich hier bewußt auf die Seite der Tradition, er versteckt die Elemente der Lichtführung nicht in der Dachkonstruktion, er hebt sie absichtsvoll heraus, dehnt die aufgesetzten Laternen fast auf Stockwerkshöhe und macht sie so zu einem selbstbewußt den Außenbau prägenden Architekturmotiv. Und da im Inneren in den Sockeln der Laternenhäuser auch die Schienen für die Zusatzbeleuchtung und die Abluftschlitze versteckt sind, bleiben die sockellos weißen Ausstellungswände von allen störenden Elementen frei; sie stellen sich fast wollüstig in den Dienst der Kunstwerke. Die Galerieräume sind also ideale Schreine für Malerei jeder Größenordnung, was dem Kernbestand der Sammlung entgegenkommt. Doch auch Skulpturen gelangen hier bestens zur Geltung. Für lichtempfindliche Grafik und für Videos aber gibt es eine Black-Box am Anfang des Rundgangs.

Dort, wo die Besucher, aus dem Foyer kommend, die Enfilade der Galerieräume betreten, liegt, noch im Eingangstrakt, die Bibliothek, eine wunderbar intime, zweigeschossige Lesestube. Die Bücherregale an den Wänden, die Arbeitstische und die um den Treppenschacht herumlaufenden Lesepulte sind alle aus einem einzigen, intensiv gemusterten Platanenstamm gefertigt, wodurch der Raum eine herrlich einheitliche Wärme erhält. Der Rest ist Glas: Eine Glaswand gibt den Blick in den ersten Galeriesaal frei, hält somit Kontakt zur Sammlung; eine begehbare, große Glasplatte im Boden der oberen Etage – sie reißt den Blick fast abrupt in die Tiefe – vermittelt in der Bücherklause zwischen oben und unten.

Der über dem Depotgeschoß gelegene Ausstellungstrakt, den die Besucher direkt vom Foyer aus betreten können oder aber am Ende der Galerieflucht erreichen, bildet architektonisch den denkbar größten Gegensatz zu seinem Pendant, dem Galerietrakt. Vom Skulpturenhof aus läßt sich die Formendramaturgie besonders eindrucksvoll studieren: auf der einen Seite die unterschiedlich weit in den Hof sich schiebenden Kuben des Galerietrakts mit den senkrechten Fensterbändern und den hohen leichten Aufbauten der Laternen, die nachts wie Lichtwürfel über dem Ganzen schweben; auf der anderen Seite ein Triumph der Waagerechten, ein langer durchfensterter Riegel, der durch eine schier endlos gedehnte Diagonale, eine langsam ansteigende Rampe, zweigeteilt wird. Über diese Rampe, die auch im Inneren der Halle als plastisches Element raumbildend wirkt, können die Besucher vom Hof aus zur Terrasse hinaufsteigen, die in ganzer Länge oben vor dem Großen Saal entlangläuft. Den Abschluß nach oben bildet das in einer sanften Welle sich aufwölbende Dach des Großen Saals, das als Reflex auf die nahen Weinberghügel gedeutet werden kann.

Vier spannungsvoll kontrastierende horizontale Linien strukturieren also den Ausstellungstrakt auf der Hofseite: die beiden Waagrechten der Stockwerksböden, die Schräge der Rampe und die Welle des Dachs. Als fünftes plastisches Element bestätigt die im Hof liegende lange Rinne aus schwarzem Basalt, in der Wasser fließt, die skulpturalen Qualitäten dieser horizontalen Architekturkomposition.

Die Ausstellungshalle, die, nur durch Querwände unterteilt, den ganzen Trakt durchläuft, erhält ihr Licht und ihr architektonisches Leben durch die beiden Längsseiten. Auf der Hofseite schwingt sich die Rampe als frei plastisches Element langsam nach oben. Unter dem langen Band der Rampe ist der Boden der Ausstellungshalle in ganzer Länge zu den Depots hinab geöffnet. Der Besucher kann dort wie von einer Empore aus hinunterschauen in jenen Bereich, der ihm beim Rundgang sonst verschlossen bleibt; ihn erreicht so eine plötzliche Ahnung von etwas, was in allen anderen Museen peinlich ausgespart bleibt: von dem riesigen Unterleib, der das illustre Leben in den Ausstellungsräumen überhaupt erst möglich macht. Daß der von Tesar als »Raumschnitt« bezeichnete Schacht beiläufig auch noch eine Menge Tageslicht in die sonst hermetisch verschlossene Unterwelt der Depots bringt, ist die nützliche Seite dieses auch bereits rein ästhetisch überzeugenden Eingriffs.

Die Trennwand zwischen Ausstellungshalle und Skulpturenhof ist also höchst ambitioniert ausgebildet. Doch die Wand, die gegenüberliegt, die Außenwand, vermag ihr auf gleichem Niveau zu antworten. Sie öffnet die Halle nicht nach unten in die Depots, sondern nach oben in den Großen Saal. Auf dieser Seite ist eine kleine Rotunde in die Halle eingestellt; sie ist nach oben offen und soll als Konzertmuschel bei Musikveranstaltungen, als Studio für elektroakustische Darbietungen oder raumbezogene Klanginstallationen beide Ausstellungsetagen miteinander verbinden. Durch das Rund ihrer Öffnung bewegt sich eine Treppe an der Außenwand nach oben. Auf halber Höhe kann der Besucher auf einem Podest haltmachen und nach innen in die Rotunde oder nach außen durch den querverlaufenden Fensterstreifen auf die Auenlandschaft und die Weinberghügel jenseits der Donau blicken.

Die untere Ausstellungshalle mit ihren Zwischenwänden und dem Gemisch aus natürlichem Seiten- und Kunstlicht hat neben den ästhetisch perfektionierten Oberlichtsälen der Galerie fast Werkstattcharakter; sie eignet sich also für alle möglichen Mischformen der Darbietung, wie sie heute im Ausstellungsbetrieb so beliebt sind, aber auch für kleinformatige Arbeiten. Im Großen Saal darüber aber, der von allen Zwischenwänden freigehalten ist – kommen die großformatigen Bilderserien und die ausladenden Objekte der Sammlung bestens zur Geltung.

Das Motiv der einbeschriebenen Rotunde paraphrasiert eines der Lieblingsmotive Tesars: das Ineinander von rechteckigen und runden Formen. Und noch eine Erinnerung taucht im Großen Saal auf: In die sanft sich aufwölbende und wieder abfallende Decke sind querrechteckige Lichtöffnungen eingelassen; sie dienen, ähnlich wie die runden Lichtkuppeln im Schömer-Haus oder in der evangelischen Kirche sowohl der formalen Belebung als auch der natürlichen Belichtung. Durch die Wölbung bekommt jeder der Lichtschlitze einen anderen Winkel zum Himmel, also auch ein anderes Licht. Und da durch das flache Fensterband in der Außen-

lem of lighting exhibition galleries in Klosterneuburg. There have been some pretty grotesque attempts to capture and direct daylight in many of the architecturally striking new museum buildings of the past thirty years. Tesar puts himself firmly on the side of tradition here. He does not hide the light control elements in the roof structure, he deliberately makes them conspicuous, stretching the lanterns on top of the building almost to the height of a full storey and thus makes them into an architectural motif that makes a self-confident impact on the exterior. And as the tracks for additional lighting and the ventilation slits are also concealed inside, in the bases of the lantern-houses, the white exhibition walls, without skirting-boards, remain free of any disturbing elements; they dedicate themselves almost sensually to serving the works of art. Thus the galleries are ideal shrines for paintings of any size, which suits the core of the collection. But sculptures can also be shown to their best advantage here. For light-sensitive graphic art and videos there is a black box at the start of the sequence of rooms .

At the point where visitors come out of the foyer and start to move through the enfilade of galleries is, still in the entrance section, the library, a wonderfully intimate, two-storey reading room. The bookshelves on the walls, the work-tables and the reading desks arranged around the stairwell are all made from a single plane-tree trunk with a very striking grain, which gives the room a wonderfully uniform warmth. The rest is glass: a glass wall makes it possible to look through to the first gallery space, and thus maintains contact with the collection; a large glass slab, on which visitors can walk, forms the floor of the upper level – it makes one look down almost abruptly – and creates a link between the upper and lower levels of the little library.

The exhibition wing above the storage floor, which visitors can enter directly from the foyer or at the end of the run of galleries, architecturally forms the greatest possible contrast with its opposite number, the gallery wing. The dramatic structure of the forms can be studied particularly impressively from the sculpture courtyard: on one side are the cubes of the gallery wing, pushing out into the courtyard to different extents, with vertical bands of windows and the high, light-weight lantern structures, floating above the whole building like cubes of light at night; on the other side is a triumph of the horizontal, a long bar with windows along its full length, cut in two by a diagonal that seems to go on for ever, a slowly rising ramp. Visitors can use this ramp, which also has the effect of a space-creating, three-dimensional element inside the hall, to go up from the courtyard to the terrace that runs the full length of the Great Hall at the top. The upper conclusion is formed by the gently rising wave of the roof of the Great Hall, which can be interpreted as a response to the nearby hills of the vineyards.

Four horizontal lines, in a tension of contrasts, thus articulate the exhibition wing on the courtyard side: the two horizontals of the floors of the storeys, the diagonal of the ramp and the wave of the roof. As a fifth three-dimensional element, the long black basalt rill in which water flows confirms the sculptural qualities of this horizontal architectural composition.

The exhibition hall is divided only by transverse walls, and runs the full length of the section. It gains its light and architectural life from the two long sides. On the courtyard side the ramps slowly climbs upwards as a free sculptural element. Under the long band of the ramp, the floor of the exhibition hall opens down to the stores along its full length. Visitors can look down from there as from a gallery at this area, which would normally be closed to them as they walk round; they are thus suddenly given an idea of something that is embarrassingly omitted in all other museums: the gigantic underbody without which the illustrious life in the exhibition rooms would not be possible at all. The shaft that Tesar calls a »spatial section« also happens to provide the otherwise closed underworld of the stores with quite a lot of light, which is the practical side of this intervention that is already convincing on purely aesthetic grounds.

So the dividing wall between the sculpture courtyard and the exhibition hall is structured very ambitiously. But the wall opposite, the outside wall, is able to respond to it on the same level. It does not open down to the space to the stores below, but upwards into the Great Hall. On this side a small rotunda is inserted into the space; it is open at the top, and is intended to link the two exhibition floors, as a concert shell at musical events, as a studio for electronic sound presentations or space-related sound installations. A flight of steps also moves upwards on the outside wall, through the round aperture. Visitors can stop on a landing half-way up and look inwards into the rotunda and outwards through the transverse strips of windows at the meadows and the hilly vineyards on the other side of the Danube.

The lower exhibition hall with its intermediate walls and a mixture of natural side-lighting and artificial light is almost workshop-like in contrast with the aesthetically perfected top-lit rooms in the gallery; it is thus suitable for all possible mixed forms of presentation of the kind that are so popular in the world of exhibitions today, but also for smaller-format works. But series of large-format pictures and the more sizeable object in the collection show to their best effect in the Great Hall above.

The motive of the inscribed rotunda is a paraphrase of one of Tesar's favourite themes: linking rectangular and circular forms. And another memory crops up in the Great Hall: transverse-rectangular light openings are let into the ceiling, which curves gently upwards and then dips down again; rather like the round light-domes in the Schömer-Haus or in the Protestant church they serve to enliven the form, but also as a source of natural light. The curve means that each of the light slits is at a different angle to the sky, and thus admits a different kind of light. And thus the Great Hall, unlike the galleries, which have totally calmed lighting, has different light situations as the shallow band of windows in the outside wall and the large French windows at the end of the inside wall admit additional light.

If visitors leave the Great Hall and move on to the long terrace, which is also used by the café, they can make an impressive comparison of the three sections surrounding the courtyard and their contrasting building forms. And from up here, standing opposite the lanterns on the gallery section, there is also a particularly beautiful view to the west of the foothills of the Vienna Woods. But to the north is the town of Klosterneuburg with the massive Chorherrenstift complex directly in view from the little round outlook cockpit; it gives visitors at least an idea of the forward-thrusting tip of the triangle of the building, of the building's con-

wand und durch die großen Fenstertüren an den Enden der Innenwand zusätzlich Licht einfällt, ergeben sich, ganz im Gegensatz zu den in der Beleuchtung völlig beruhigten Galerieräumen, im Großen Saal verschiedene Lichtsituationen, die den Raum atmosphärisch aufteilen und beleben.

Tritt man aus dem Saal hinaus auf die lange Terrasse, die auch vom Café genutzt wird, kann man nicht nur die drei den Hof rahmenden Trakte in ihren gegensätzlichen Bauformen eindrucksvoll miteinander vergleichen, es tut sich von hier oben, wo man den Laternen des Galerietrakts gegenübersteht, auch ein besonders schöner Blick nach Westen auf die Ausläufer des Wienerwalds auf. Im Norden aber liegt die Stadt Klosterneuburg mit dem gewaltigen Massiv des Stifts direkt im Blickfeld der kleinen runden Aussichtskanzel; sie gibt dem Besucher wenigstens eine Ahnung von der vorgeschobenen Spitze des Gebäudedreiecks, von der architektonisch höchst eigenwillig ausgeprägten Abschlußgeste des Hauses in Richtung Stadt.

Wie so oft in seinen Bauten, etwa am Vordach des Schömer-Hauses, läßt Tesar eine der Außenlinien über das geometrische Grundgerüst hinauslaufen und in einem kurvigen Zipfel, einem gebauten Schnörkel enden. Hier, beim Museum, münden die beiden nach Norden zielenden geraden Außenwände jeweils in eine Kurve: Die westliche Wand endet in einem kleinen runden Erker, der im oberen Ausstellungsgeschoß als Terrasse nutzbar ist; die östliche Wand läuft mit einem schmalen Gebäudestreifen noch ein ganzes Stück weiter nach Norden, schwenkt dann in mehreren Brüchen nach innen und bildet so einen quasi geschuppten, spitz endenden Gebäudezipfel, der sich im Charakter deutlich von der geschlossenen Masse des Museumsbaus unterscheidet. Er umschreibt mit seiner einwärts gedrehten Geste eine Art Binnenhof, einen angedeuteten, magisch aufgeladenen Raum, den der Architekt als Rosengarten gestaltet und mit einer seiner skulpturalen Arbeiten besetzt hat.

Dieser kapriziöse Tesar-Schnörkel ist formal wie inhaltlich deutlich vom Dreieck der übrigen Trakte abgesetzt. Man könnte ihn als die architektonische Kür nach Absolvierung der Pflicht einstufen. Das Hauptgeschoß endet an der Nordspitze in einem großzügigen Konferenzraum. Ihm kommen die beiden Architekturausleger zugute. In den mit schmalen Fensterschlitzen versehenen Runderker ist eine Sitznische hineinmodelliert, die zu entspanntem Plaudern einlädt. Der nach Norden ausschreitende, am Ende schneckenartig gewendelte Anbau aber bewährt sich als angenehm heller Besprechungsraum. Seine geknickte Spitze ist an den Knickstellen mit jeweils senkrechten Fensterstreifen versehen, die zwangsläufig jeweils in eine andere Richtung zielen und so den kleinen Wurmfortsatz zu einer einprägsamen, aller Nützlichkeit enthobenen, vom Licht und von der Aussicht bestimmten Raumfigur machen. Im Stockwerk darüber, in der Höhe des Großen Saals, ist über dem Konferenzraum ein privates Arbeitszimmer für Karlheinz Essl eingerichtet. Und wie beim Erker dient auch hier der ausscherende Annex als Terrasse. Der Stifter kann hier also mit seinen Gästen und Künstlerfreunden auf eine weit vorgestreckte, dem Museumsbetrieb entzogene Kanzel hinaustreten und den schönen Rundumblick auf die Landschaft und die Stadt genießen.

Wäre Essl vom österreichischen Staat in das neue Museumsquartier in den Wiener Hofstallungen eingeladen worden, hätte er seine Sammlung mit den kaiserlichen Hinterlassenschaften, mit den berühmten Museen am Ring messen können. In Klosterneuburg kann er nun im eigenen Haus selbstbewußt dem ähnlich großartigen Baukomplex des Chorherrenstifts gegenübertreten. Hier fehlen zwar die musealen Vergleichsmaßstäbe, die den Rang seiner Sammlung bestätigen würden, doch der Soloauftritt im architektonisch eigenwilligen, mit allen museologischen Finessen bestückten Baukomplex wirkt noch um einiges ausdrucksvoller als die Einbindung in die staatlichen Sammlungen.

Der Trotz, der mit im Spiel gewesen sein dürfte, als die Essls sich von der Wiener Vision verabschiedeten und zu einem eigenen Museumsbau entschlossen, er hat in der nach außen fast abweisenden Klosterneuburger Museumsarchitektur seine symbolische Ausformung gefunden. Daß die drei exponierten Eckpunkte des Stiftungsbollwerks wie die Türme einer Burg jeweils für ein anderes Mitglied der Familie bestimmt sind, das ist nicht nur ein sichtbares Zeichen für das gewachsene Selbstbewußtsein der Stifter, es zeigt auch, wie direkt Agnes und Karlheinz Essl sowie ihr komponierender Sohn das künstlerische Leben in der Stiftung mitbestimmen wollen, wie entschieden sie die Spielwiese des Hauses als eines ihrer Arbeitsfelder betrachten.

Die drei familiären Arbeitsräume über dem Kulturzentrum lassen den privaten Charakter der Stiftung also keinen Zweifel aufkommen. Doch die Funktionen des Museums werden durch das ausgespannte Kräftenetz nirgendwo eingeschränkt. Der Besucher spürt von den organisatorischen Hintergründen wenig, er erlebt die Präsentation der Sammlung als reinen Glücksfall, die Architektur aber als ein ästhetisches Abenteuer, als Erfüllung mancher Wünsche, die von anderen neuen Museumsbauten geweckt, aber nicht erfüllt wurden.

Heinz Tesar hat die künstlerischen Freiheiten, die ihm der Bauherr einräumte, genutzt und intensiv nach Lösungen für jene Probleme gesucht, die bei öffentlichen Museumsbauten oft nur angedacht werden. So wird sein Haus für die Sammlung Essl nicht nur in seinem eigenen Œuvre einen prominenten Platz einnehmen, es wird auch in der keineswegs langweiligen Geschichte des neueren Museumsbaus eine bedeutende Rolle spielen.

Vor allem mit seinen vielfältigen Methoden der Lichtzufuhr und seinen wechselnden Raumfiguren für die Auftrittsrituale der zeitgenössischen Kunst hat Tesar Maßstäbe gesetzt. Seine ausgeklügelte Variante der klassischen Oberlichtlaterne und sein leicht zu bedienendes Aufbewahrungssystem für Bilder sollten zum Lernprogramm aller Hochschulen gehören. Insgesamt ist es aber wohl das zwanglose und doch höchst sinnfällige In- und Nebeneinander der verschiedenen Museumsfunktionen, das den Reiz der kompakten Raumkomposition in Klosterneuburg ausmacht.

Tesars Museumsbau schafft etwas, was eigentlich ein Widerspruch ist: Er stellt sich ganz in den Dienst der ausgestellten Kunstwerke und profiliert sich gerade mit dieser Besonderheit als architektonisches Individuum, als autonomes Bau-Kunstwerk. Mit seiner enigmatischen Erscheinung läßt er etwas von jenem Geheimnis ahnen, das den Künsten eigentlich immer zu eigen sein sollte, das in den letzten Jahrzehnten aber – auch durch allzu aufgeregte Museumsarchitekturen – oft verspielt worden ist.

cluding gesture towards the town, which bears a most unconventional stamp in architectural terms.

Tesar, as he so often does in his buildings, in the canopy of the Schömer-Haus, for example, allows one of the outside lines to run out of the basic geometrical framework and end in a curved tip, a built flourish. Here, in the museum, the two north-pointing, straight walls each end in a curve: the west wall in a little rounded bay that can be used as a terrace on the upper exhibition floor; the east wall continues quite a lot further north in the form of a narrow strip of building, then swings inwards in several breaks and thus forms a more or less scaled tip for the building ending in a point, which is clearly different in character from the closed mass of the museum building. Its inward-turning gesture surrounds a kind of inner courtyard, an indicated, magically charged space that the architect has designed as a rose garden and has placed one of his sculptures in it.

This capricious flourish by Tesar is clearly set apart from the triangle of the other sections in terms of both form and content. It could be categorized as a piece of architectural treatment in a spa after one's duty has been done. The main floor ends in a generously sized conference room at its northern tip. It benefits from both the architectural outriggers. Modelled into the round bay, which has narrow window slits, is a niche for sitting that invites visitors to relax and chat. But the extension to the building that moves out towards the north, spiralling like a snail at the end, holds its own as a pleasantly light meeting-room. Its indented tip has narrow vertical window-strips at each kink, which inevitably all point in different directions and thus make the little worm-like continuation into a memorable spatial figure, not serving any practical purpose and defined by light and the view. On the upper floor, at the level of the Great Hall, Karlheinz Essl has his own study above the conference room. And as in the case of the bay, the annexe that breaks out at this point also serves as a terrace. The man who gave all this to the town can thus step out with this guests and artist friends on to a cockpit that thrusts well forward and is away from the business of the museum, and enjoy the beautiful panoramic view of the countryside and the town.

If Essl had been invited by the Austrian state into the new museum quarter in the court stables in Vienna he would have been able to measure his collection against the legacy of the empire, the famous museums on the Ring. In Klosterneuburg he can stand in his own building and confidently face the similarly magnificent complex of buildings that make up the Chorherrenstift. Certainly there are no comparisons here in the form of museums to confirm the status of his collection, but the solo appearance in a building complex that is architecturally unconventional and fitted out with every possible item of museum finesse seems considerably more impressive that being tied in with the state collections.

The defiance that must have come into play when the Essls said goodbye to the Vienna vision and decided to build their own museum has found symbolic form in the architecture of the Klosterneuburg museum, which is almost forbidding from the outside. The fact that the three exposed corner points of the foundation's bastion, like the towers of a castle, are each intended for a different member of the family is not just a visible sign of the founder's mature self-confidence.

It also shows that Agnes and Karlheinz Essl and their composer son intend to keep to shape the artistic life of the foundation, and how definitely they see the playground offered by the building as a field in which they want to work.

And so the three workrooms for the members of the family above the culture centre leave no doubt about the private character of the foundation. But the functions of the museum are not restricted at any point by the outstretched network of forces. Visitors have little sense of the organization going on in the background, they experience the presentation of the collection as a happy chance, but the architecture as an aesthetic adventure, as the fulfilment of many a desire that has been awoken by other new museum buildings, but not satisfied.

Heinz Tesar has made full use of the artistic liberties allowed him by his client, and sought intensively for solutions that for all the problems that are often only half considered in public museum buildings. Thus his building for the Essl Collection will not only occupy a prominent place in his own œuvre, it will also play an important part in the by no means boring story of recent museum architecture.

Tesar has set standards above all with his many methods for providing light and his changing spatial configurations for the appearance rituals of contemporary art. His ingenious variation on the classical top-light lantern and his easy-to-use method for storing pictures should be part of the course at all institutes of higher education. But overall it is probably the free-and-easy and yet highly intelligent linking and juxtaposition of the various museum functions that explain the charm of this compact spatial composition in Klosterneuburg.

Tesar's museum building creates something that is actually a contradiction: it puts itself entirely at the service of the works of art exhibited, and establishes itself as an architectural individual, as a built work of art in its own right with precisely this special feature. Its enigmatic appearance gives some idea of the mystery that should always be part of the arts, but that has often been squandered in recent decades by some unduly agitated museum architecture.

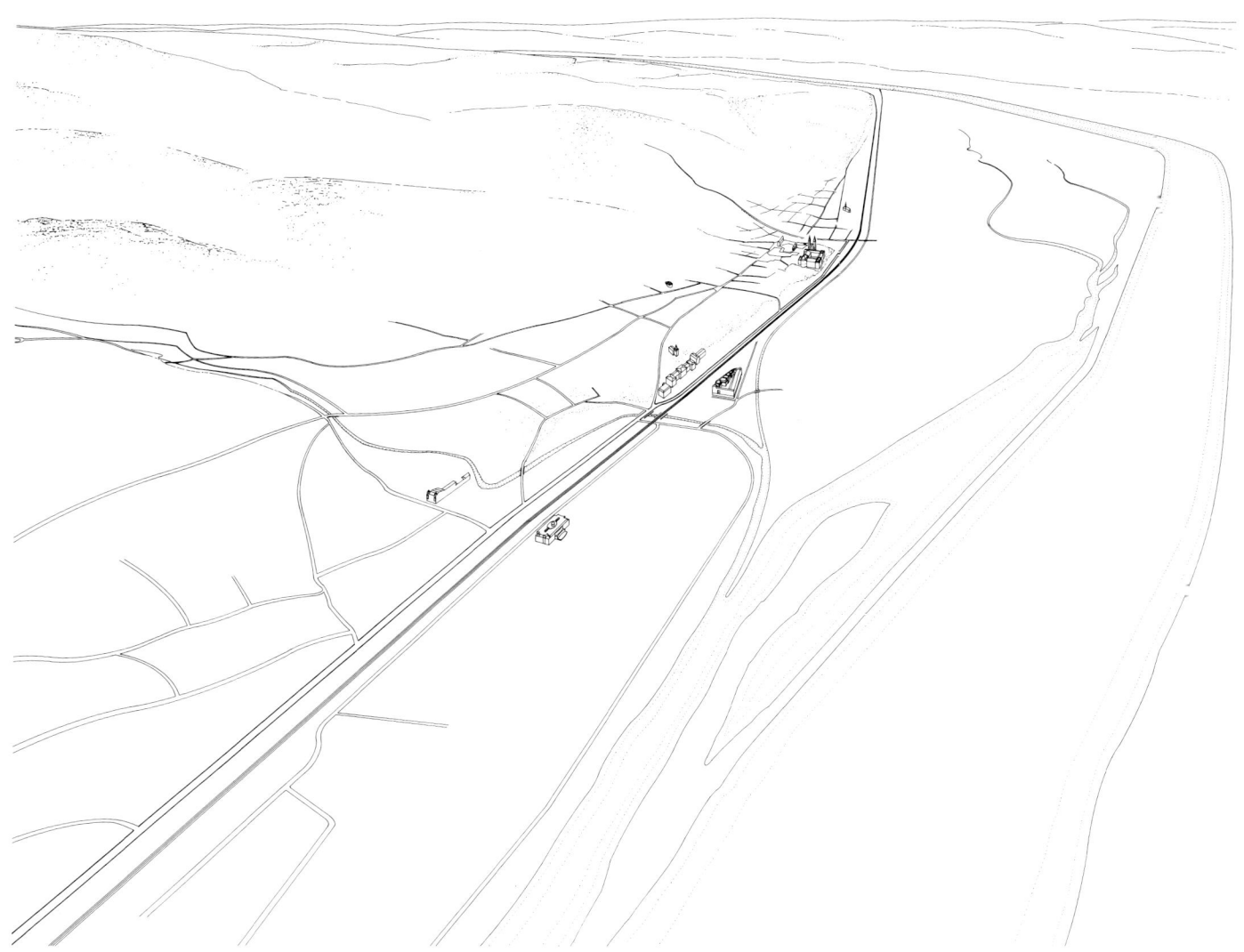

1. Perspekive der Gesamtsituation.
2. Lageplan.

1. Perspective view of the general situation.
2. Site plan.

S. 180, 181
3–6. Grundrisse (Ebenen 0/1, 2/3, 4/5) und Dachaufsicht).

p. 180, 181
3–6. Floor plans (levels 0/1, 2/3, 4/5) and top view.

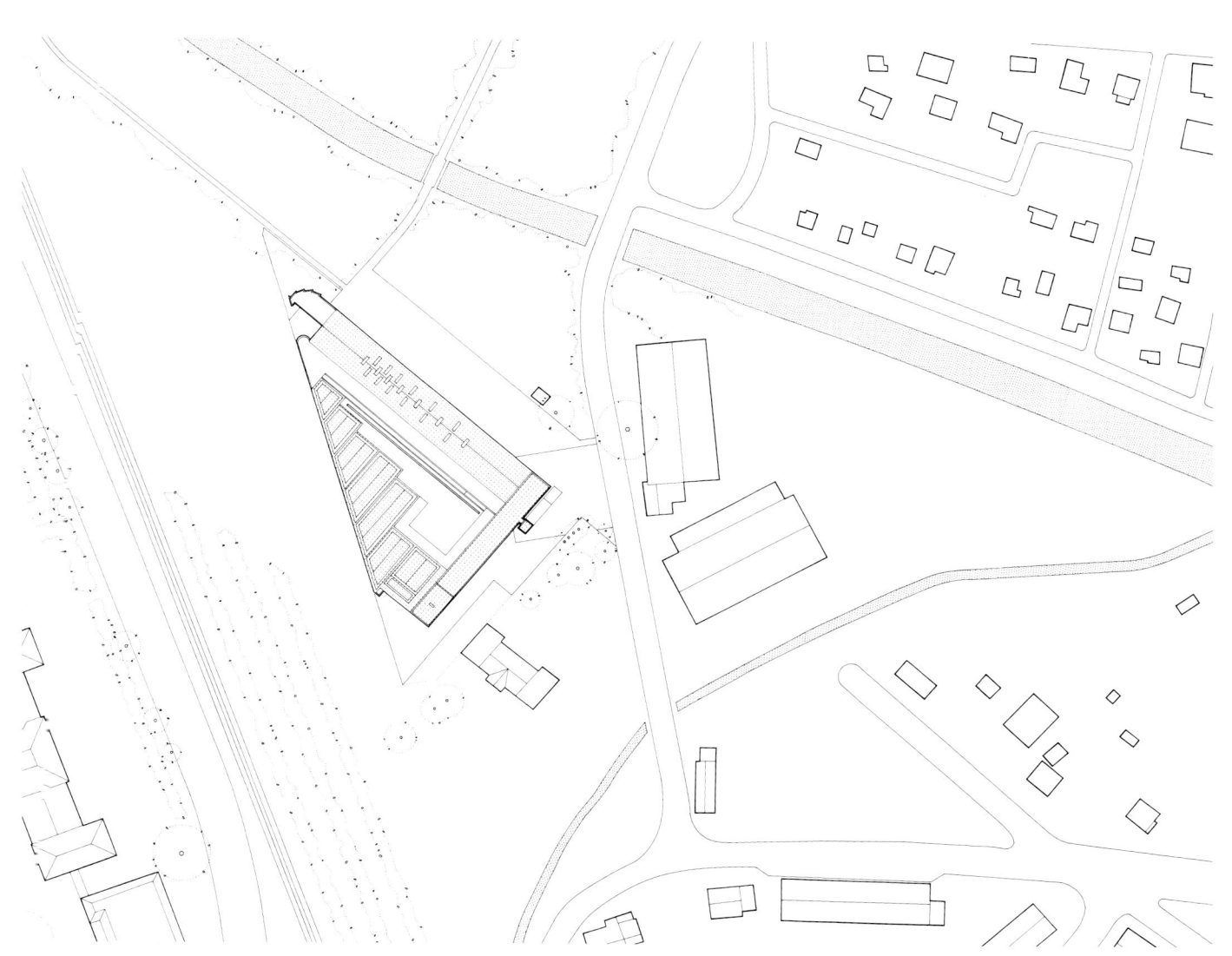

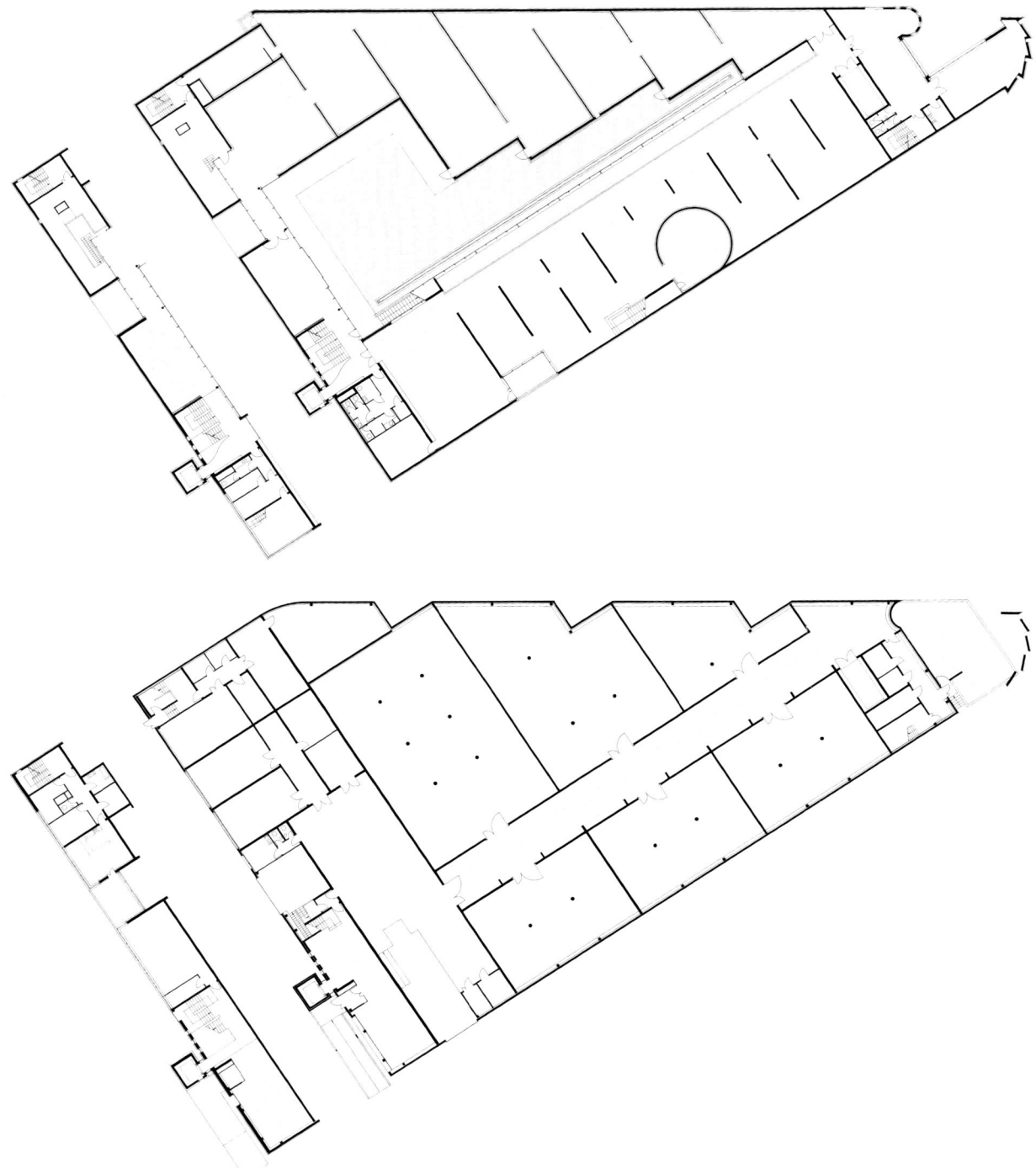

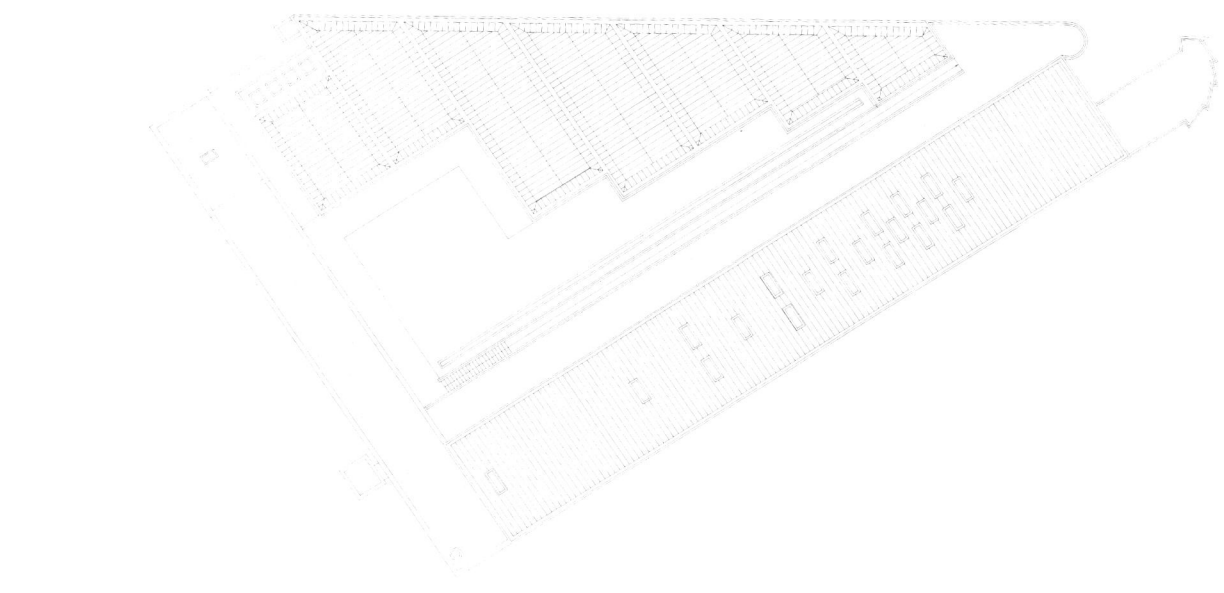
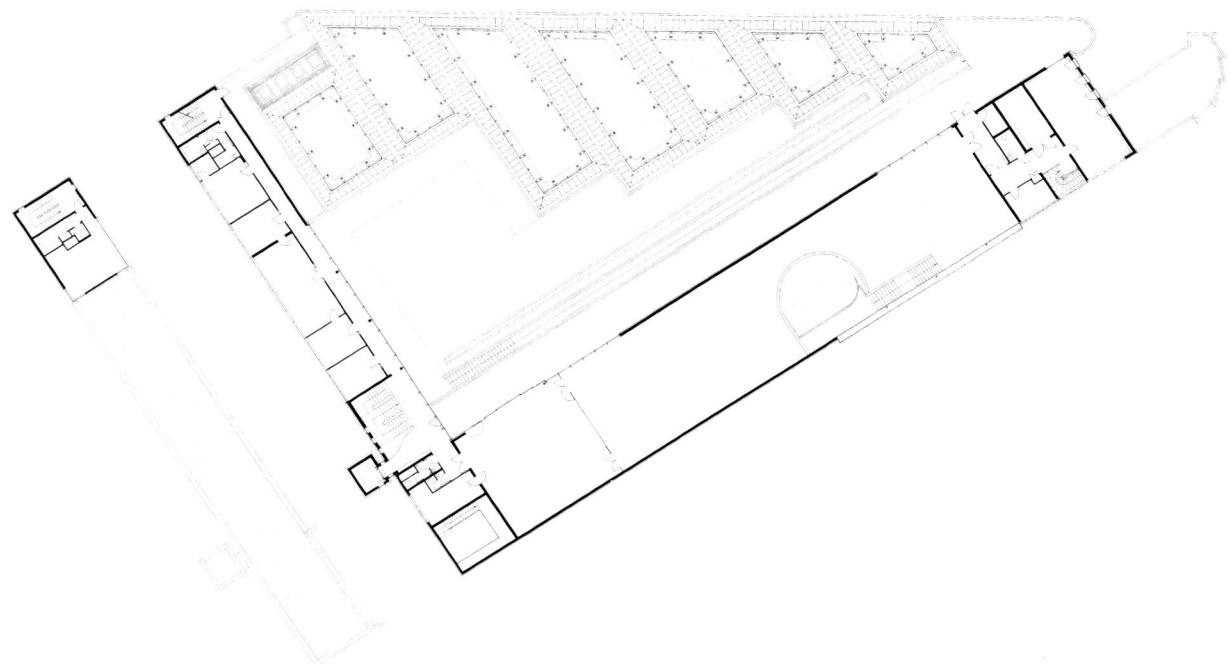

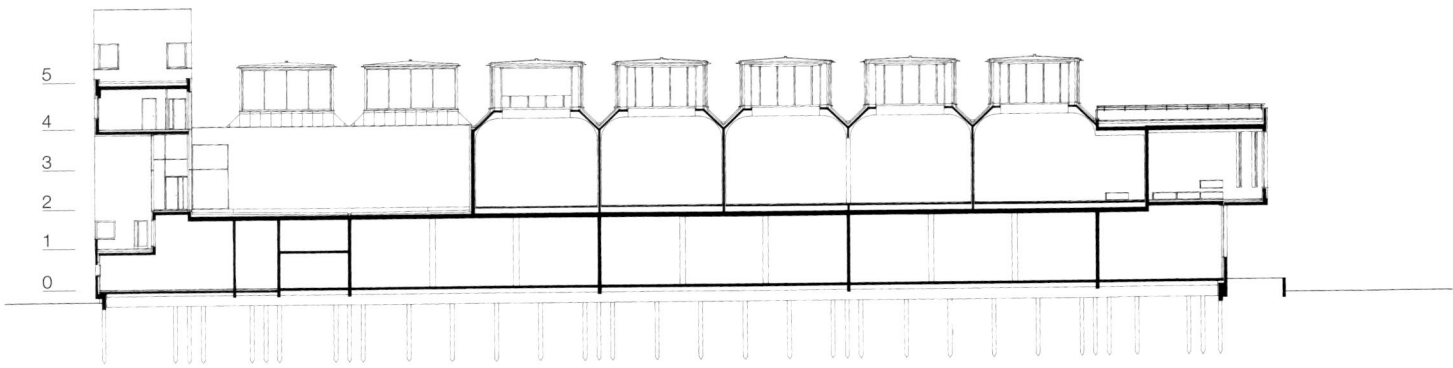

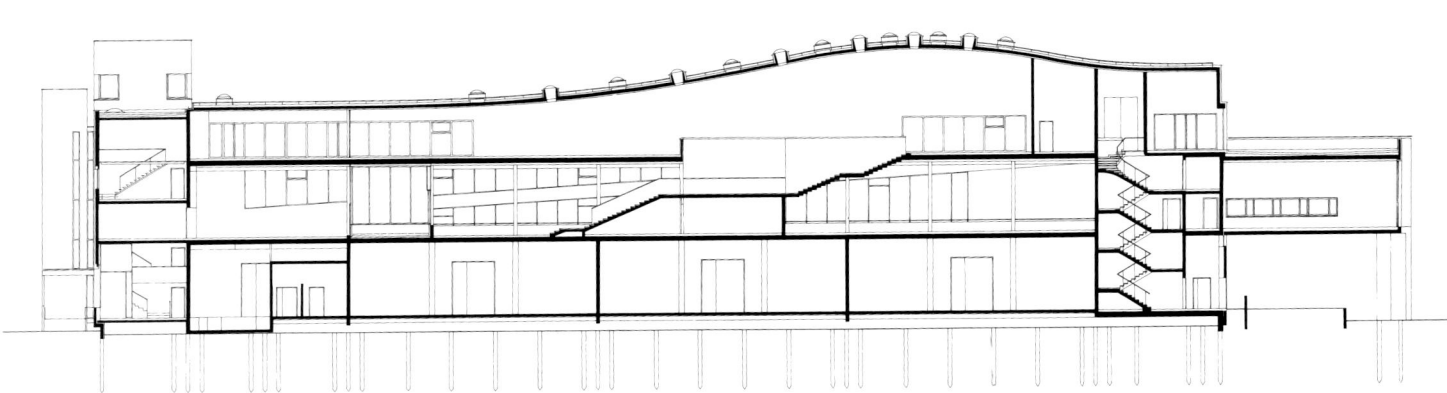

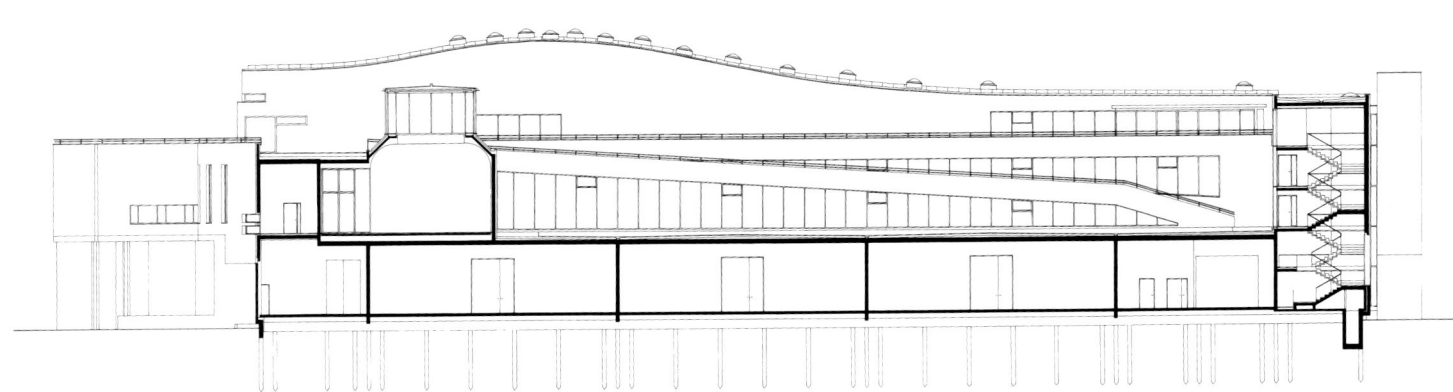

7–12. Schnitte und Aufrisse.

7–12. Sections and elevations.

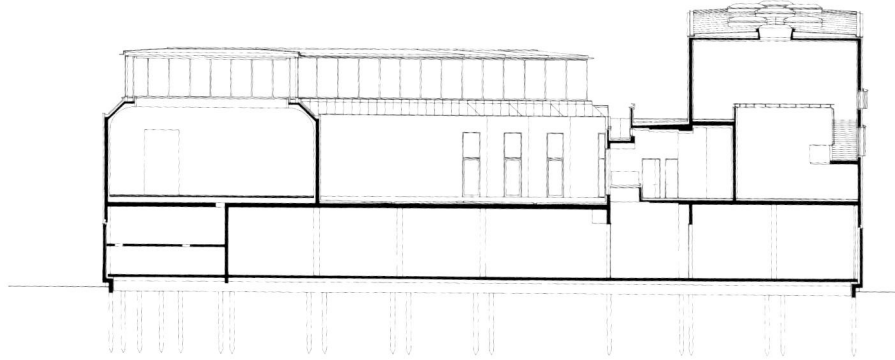

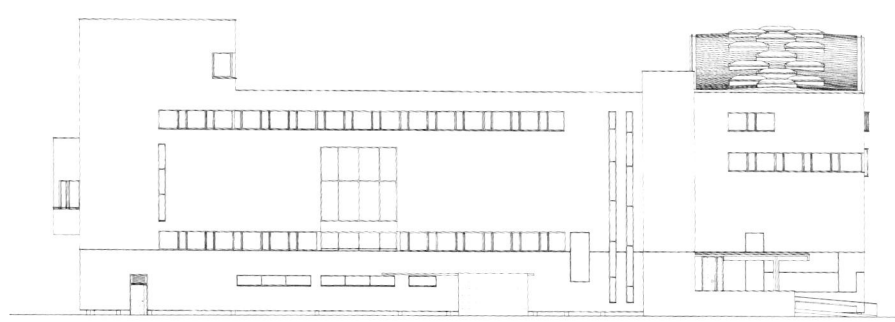

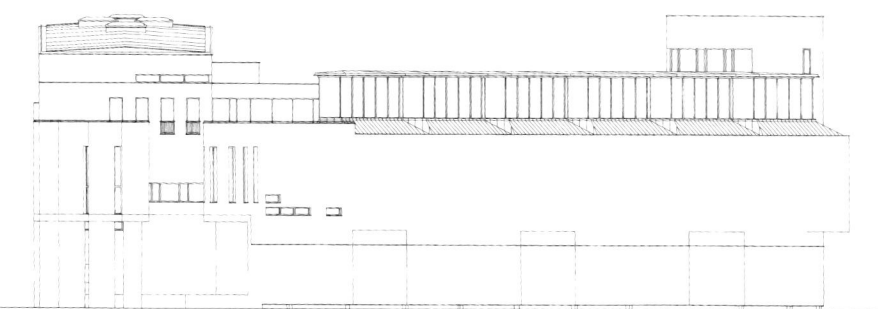

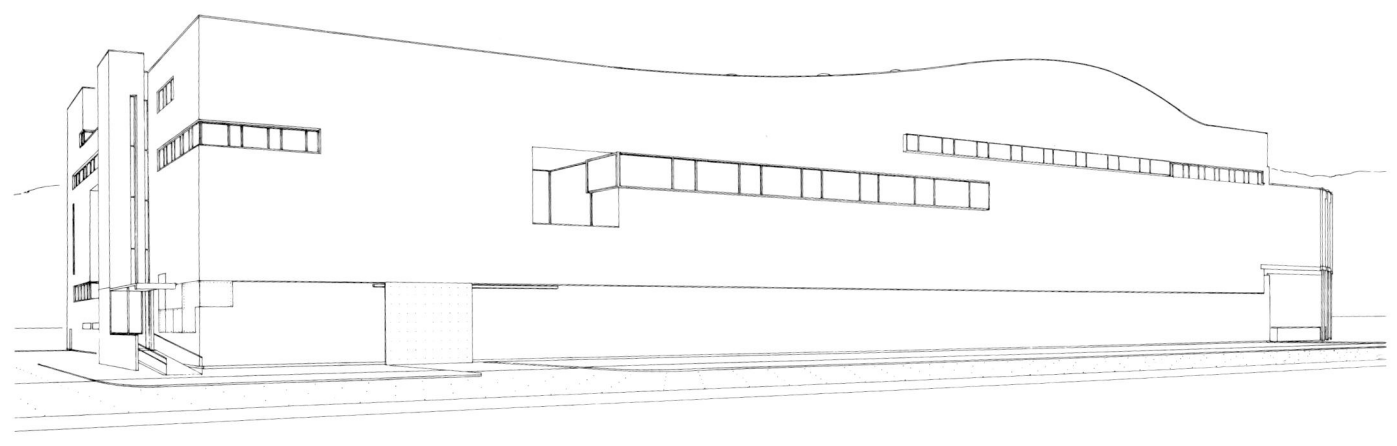

13, 14. Perspektiven.
13, 14. Perspectve views.

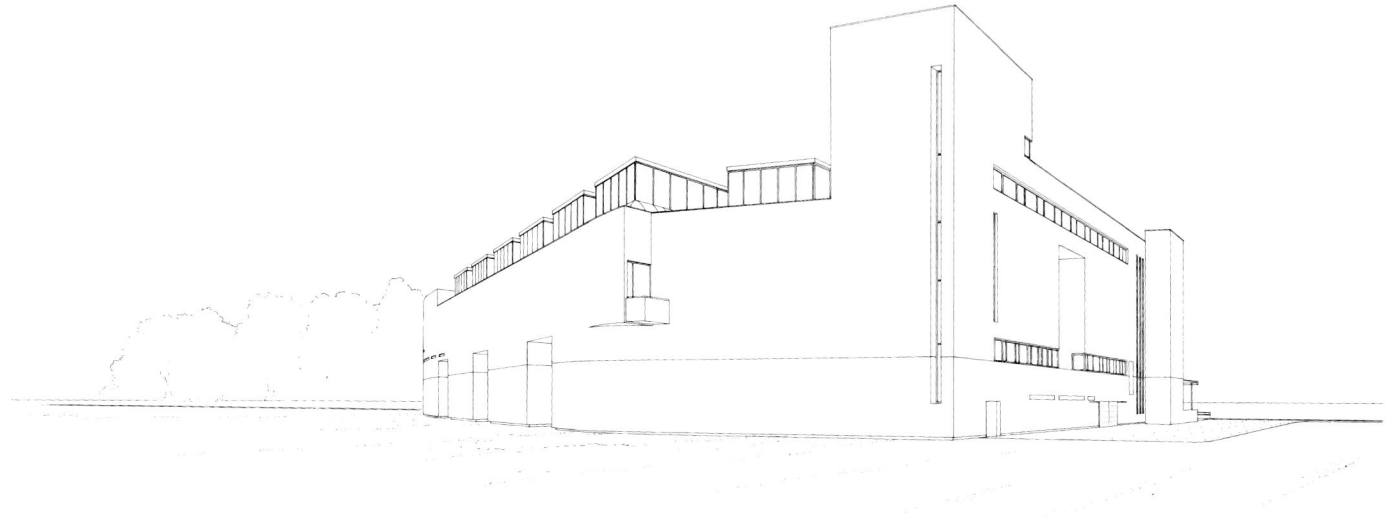

S. 186/187
1. Gesamtansicht von Nordwesten. Im Hintergrund die Stadt Wien mit den Türmen der Donau City.

p. 186/187
1. General view from the northwest. In the background the city of Vienna with the towers of the Donau City.

2. Gesamtansicht von Nordwesten.
3. Gesamtansicht von Süden.
4. Gesamtansicht von Südwesten.

2. General view from the northwest.
3. General view from the south.
4. General view from the southwest.

S. 190/191
5. Gesamtansicht von Westen.

p. 190/191
5. General view from the west.

6. Gesamtansicht von Osten mit Hauptzugang.
7. Gesamtansicht von Norden.

6. General view from the east with main entrance.
7. General view from the north.

S. 194, 195
8. Detailansicht von Osten.
9. Detailansicht von Norden.

p. 194, 195
8. Detailed view from the east.
9. Detailed view from the north.

S. 196, 197
10, 11. Detailansichten der nördlichen Spitze des Gebäudes.

p. 196, 197
10, 11. Detailed views of the north corner of the building.

S. 198, 199
12, 13. Detailansichten der östlichen Spitze des Gebäudes mit Hauptzugang.

p. 198, 199
12, 13. Detailed views of the east corner of the building with main entrance.

14, 15. Das Haupttreppenhaus.

14, 15. The main staircase.

16. Der Innenhof. Links der Galerietrakt, rechts der Ausstellungstrakt.
17, 18. Detailansichten der Laternen auf dem Galerietrakt.

16. The courtyard. The gallery wing to the left, the exhibition wing to the right.
17, 18. Detailed views of the lanterns on the gallery wing.

205

S. 204, 205
19. Der Galerietrakt mit Gemälden von Karel Appel, Georg Baselitz und Otto Zitko.
20. Der Galerietrakt mit Gemälden von Emilio Vedova und Asger Jorn.

p. 204, 205
19. The gallery wing with paintings by Karel Appel, Georg Baselitz and Otto Zitko.
20. The gallery wing with paintings by Emilio Vedova and Asger Jorn.

21. Der Galerietrakt mit Gemälden von Per Kirkeby, Max Weiler und Asger Jorn.
22. Der Galerietrakt mit Gemälden von Georg Baselitz, Karel Appel und Per Kirkeby.

21. The gallery wing with paintings by Per Kirkeby, Max Weiler and Asger Jorn.
22. The gallery wing with paintings by Georg Baselitz, Karel Appel and Per Kirkeby.

23. Der Galerietrakt mit Gemälden von Maria Lassnig, Peter Kogler, Pierre Soulages sowie Skulpturen von Marc Quinn und Fritz Wotruba.
24. Der Galerietrakt mit Gemälden von Pierre Soulages und Emilio Vedova sowie einer Skulptur von Fritz Wotruba.

23. The gallery wing with paintings by Maria Lassnig, Peter Kogler, Pierre Soulages and skulptures by Marc Quinn and Fritz Wotruba.
24. The gallery wing with paintings by Pierre Soulages and Emilio Vedova and a sculpture by Fritz Wotruba.

25, 26. Das untere Geschoß des Ausstellungstraktes mit Gemälden von Wolfgang Hollegha, Dieter Roth, Hans Staudacher und Martin Kippenberger.

25, 26. The lower floor of the exhibition wing with paintings by Wolfgang Hollegha, Dieter Roth, Hans Staudacher and Martin Kippenberger.

27. Das untere Geschoß des Ausstellungstraktes mit Skulpturen von Mimmo Palladino und Franz West.
28. Die über zwei Geschosse reichende »Rotunde« im Ausstellungstrakt.

27. The lower floor of the exhibition wing with sculptures by Mimmo Palladino and Franz West.
28. The two-storey »rotunda« in the exhibition wing.

S. 214/215
29. Der Große Saal im oberen Geschoß des Ausstellungstraktes mit Gemälden von Markus Lüpertz und Gilbert & George sowie Skulpturen von Nam June Paik, Jannis Kounellis und Markus Lüpertz.

p. 214/215
29. The Great Hall on the upper floor of the exhibition wing with paintings by Markus Lüpertz and Gilbert & George and sculptures by Nam June Paik, Jannis Kounellis and Markus Lüpertz.

30, 31. Der Große Saal mit Gemälden von Markus Lüpertz und Gilbert & George sowie einer Skulptur von Markus Lüpertz.
30, 31. The Great Hall with a painting by Markus Lüpertz and Gilbert & George and a sculpture by Markus Lüpertz.

32, 33. Das Depot.

32, 33. The storage area.

S. 220/221
34. Gesamtansicht von Südwesten bei Nacht.

p. 220/221
34. General view from the southwest at night.

**Sammlung Essl
Klosterneuburg
An der Donau-Au 1**

Bauherr / Clients
Fritz Schömer GmbH, Klosterneuburg

Architekt / Architect
Heinz Tesar, Wien / Vienna
Projektleitung / Project management: Susanne Veit
Mitarbeiter / Collaborators: Oliver Aschenbrenner,
Ruedi Bühlmann, Urs Geiger, Kathrin Grumböck,
Johann Osterrieder, Silvia Prager, Franz Steinberger,
Marc Tesar

Projektsteuerung / Project management
Pörner + Partner, Wien / Vienna

Statik / Statics
Christian Aste, Innsbruck

Haustechnik / Mechanical engineering
Euconsult GmbH, Wien / Vienna

Lichtplanung / Lighting design
Charles Keller Design AG, St. Gallen

Klimatechnik / Air-conditioning
PME Technisches Büro für Klimatechnik GmbH,
Ollern, Niederösterreich

Bauphysik / Structural physics
Walter Prause, Wien / Vienna

Bauunternehmen / Main contractor
Ing. E. Auböck GmbH, Enns, Oberösterreich

Möblierung / Furnishing
Vitra GmbH, Wien / Vienna
Ing. Gerhard Graschopf GmbH, Gresten, Niederösterreich